COSMIC TRENDS

Astrology Connects the Dots

About the Author

Philip Brown has written several articles on the astrology of cultural and political trends that have appeared in *The Mountain Astrologer*, *The International Astrologer*, and *Llewellyn's Starview Almanac 2006*. He is a member of the American Federation of Astrologers, the International Society for Astrological Research, and the National Council for Geocosmic Research.

Brown received his Master of Arts degree in English from California State University, Los Angeles. For the past twenty years, he has been an English teacher. He has received numerous recognitions as an educator, and was given the Golden Apple award for his work serving economically disadvantaged students in the Los Angeles area.

Brown lives in Ventura County, California, with his wife, teenage daughter, two cats, and a dog.

For more information, please visit Philip Brown's website and blog at http://www.AstroFutureTrends.com.

Philip
BROWN

COSMIC TRENDS

Astrology Connects the Dots

Llewellyn Publications
Woodbury, Minnesota

FIRST EDITION
First Printing, 2006

Book design by Tanya Filitz and Rebecca Zins

Cover design by Gavin Dayton Duffy

Cover images © Photodisc, DigitalVision, ComStock,
Corel Professional Photos, brandX, and SuperStock;
interior images by the Llewellyn Art Department

Editing by Brett Fechheimer

Chart wheels were produced by the Kepler program by permission
of Cosmic Patterns Software, Inc. (www.AstroSoftware.com)

Excerpts from "American Denim: Blue Jeans and Their Multiple Layers of Meaning," by
Beverly Gordon, from *Dress and Popular Culture* by Patricia A. Cunningham.
Reprinted by permission of The University of Wisconsin Press.

Portions of this book originally appeared in *The Mountain Astrologer.*

Llewellyn is a registered trademark of Llewellyn Worldwide, Ltd.

Cover model(s) used for illustrative purposes only and
may not endorse or represent the book's subject.

LIBRARY OF CONGRESS CATALOGING-IN-PUBLICATION DATA

Brown, Philip, 1948-
Cosmic trends: astrology connects the dots / Philip Brown.—1st ed.
p. cm.
Includes bibliographical references (p.) and index.
ISBN-13: 978-0-7387-0992-5
ISBN-10: 0-7387-0992-1
1. Astrology. I. Title.

BF1708.1.B75 2006
133.5—dc22

2006048652

Llewellyn Worldwide does not participate in, endorse, or have any authority or responsibility concerning private business transactions between our authors and the public.

All mail addressed to the author is forwarded but the publisher cannot, unless specifically instructed by the author, give out an address or phone number.

Any Internet references contained in this work are current at publication time, but the publisher cannot guarantee that a specific location will continue to be maintained. Please refer to the publisher's website for links to authors' websites and other sources.

Llewellyn Publications
A Division of Llewellyn Worldwide, Ltd.
2143 Wooddale Drive, Dept. 0-7387-0992-1
Woodbury, MN 55125-2989, U.S.A.
www.llewellyn.com

Printed in the United States of America

To my wife, Karin

Contents

Part IV—Seeing the Big Picture: Planet Cycles and Major Trends

Acknowledgments

I'd like to thank Llewellyn Worldwide for accepting my manuscript held together with a rubber band and transforming it into a real book. I am grateful to everyone involved in the publishing process at Llewellyn, but I'd like to acknowledge in particular Stephanie Clement for shepherding my book through the acquisitions process; annuals editor Sharon Leah; Becky Zins and Tanya Filitz for the overall book design; Gavin Duffy for the eye-catching cover; and especially Brett Fechheimer, editor extraordinaire.

I owe a huge debt of gratitude to the astrologers who have built a powerful foundation of astrological knowledge over the years, decades, and centuries. This book was made possible only by their foundation of accumulated knowledge. Also contributing to this book were the modern communities of astrologers who selflessly share their knowledge and wisdom.

I'd like to thank Nan Geary and Tem Tarriktar of *The Mountain Astrologer*. I am grateful for their support.

Thanks to my mother, Sally, for giving me an unquenchable thirst to explore the unknown; and to my father, Dave, who taught me the values of patience and tolerance.

I'd like to give a special acknowledgement to Cheri, who helped to uncover a book inside of me; and Chuck, who understands how some things work when I haven't got a clue.

And especially, thanks to my wife Karin, whose patience and encouragement were invaluable in the writing of this book. She's been a partner, a sounding board, and an inspiration. I couldn't have done it without you, sweetheart. And to my daughter, Lisa, who taught me what it means to grow young and see the world through beautiful Pluto in Scorpio eyes: you are a joy.

A Note About Pluto

As it does for Saturn, Uranus, and Neptune, this book explores the astrological meaning and significance of Pluto—the planet named after the Roman god of the underworld. Astrology has attached significance to the deep symbolism of the planets, as well as to their astrophysical features, and astrologers often find synchronous connections between the symbolic and astronomical qualities of the planets.

Pluto recently experienced a scientific redefinition, from full-fledged planet to "dwarf planet," but for astrologers Pluto's symbolic power remains undimmed. Ever since Pluto was first discovered in 1930, and was subsequently incorporated into horoscopes by astrologers, it has proven to be one of the most reliable indicators and predictors of generational traits, events in individual lives, and trends in the larger world. Its recent redefinition has not reduced its power in astrology, just as a champion tennis player's switch to a lighter racket need not lessen the power of the player's serve.

Pluto's unique astrological power is symbolized by, among other features, its highly elliptical orbit and its singular connection to its own moon.

Pluto does not orbit our sun in a neat circle, but rather it moves slowly in an elongated oval, as though an unseen hand were stretching its path. Its egg-shaped orbit brings it from deep within the Kuiper Belt (a ring of small objects rotating at the outer edges of the solar system far beyond Neptune and believed to be the source of comets[1]) to a point where it is actually inside Neptune's orbit. Pluto's orbit is like a gentle cosmic lasso thrown over the outer limits of our solar system, connecting the planets to the collective celestial bodies of the Kuiper Belt.

Pluto's moon, Charon, is named after the boatman in Greek mythology who ferried the dead across the river Acheron. Unlike Earth's moon, which has its own center of gravity, Pluto's center of gravity is in the space midway between it and Charon.[2] Pluto and Charon rotate while eternally facing one another, locked in a cosmic embrace, and Pluto is mythically empowered by its gravitational connection to its moon, the ferryman of the dead.

No matter how it is classified in new astronomy texts, Pluto's symbolic power will continue to resonate deep within our individual psyches and in the cosmic trends of which we are all a part.

Endnotes

1. David Jewitt, "Kuiper Belt," http://www.ifa.hawaii.edu/~jewitt/kb.html (accessed 28 August 2006).
2. S. Alan Stern, "About Pluto-Charon," *The Pluto Portal*, http://www.plutoportal.net/aboutplutocharon.htm (accessed 28 August 2006).

Introduction

At the dawn of the twenty-first century, the planets are poised to usher in an era of both great promise and peril. Powerful astrological influences are being felt throughout the world. Transformational Pluto is completing a cycle of almost 250 years. In 2008, it will return to the same zodiac sign where it was when the first sparks of the American Revolution were kindled. Neptune and Uranus, the planets of dreams and freedom, recently joined together in the heavens for the first time in over 170 years. Then these two planets "traded signs," intensifying the sharing of planetary energies and affecting our lives in everything from iPods to *I, Robot*. The merging energies of Jupiter and Saturn are also changing our world in dramatic ways.

Most people who first look into astrology are attracted by its uncanny ability to give us unique insight into our own lives and personalities. However, astrology can also be used to provide us with singular insight into the world around us—the movies and TV shows we watch, the music we listen to, the clothes we wear, and where we are going as a society and as a nation. *Cosmic Trends* is about how to use the language of astrological cycles and the slow movement of the outer planets to see cosmic patterns reflected in everything and everyone.

Astrology is not a psychic hotline, but it is a symbolic language with future tenses. One of these future tenses, planetary cycles, can help us to understand evolving social trends and cultural transformation. In this book, you will discover how the planets are already having a startling impact—from basketball to biogenetics, from Harry Potter to Hummers—on our twenty-first century lives.

As a culture, we are deluged with an endless parade of unpredictable events, trends, icons, and fashions. In the last thirty years, humanity has produced more information than in the previous five thousand. About one thousand books are published worldwide every *day*, and the total of printed knowledge doubles every five years. The average American sees sixteen thousand advertisements, logos, and labels in a day.[1]

Cosmic Trends will show you how to use astrology to make sense of this fragmented world and understand the warp-speed changes taking place around us.

Only by stepping back and looking at the big planetary picture can we begin to see astrological connections between clothing styles and best-selling books or the planetary synchronicities that connect nostalgia and Nirvana. *Cosmic Trends* will show you how . . .

- the outer planets can be understood in ways that affect us all.
- major planet conjunctions indicate important trends and future directions in our culture.
- Pluto, Neptune, and Uranus are already having a startling impact on our twenty-first century lives.
- you can prepare for the future by understanding the meaning of the outer planets' next phases.

Pluto, Neptune, and Uranus are important when looking at cultural change because they move slowly enough through the heavens to have a pronounced effect on cultural trends here on earth. Uranus takes about seven years to go through one sign of the zodiac, Neptune fourteen years, and Pluto anywhere from twelve to over thirty.

The effects of planets on our shared lives are like waves hitting a sandy shoreline. Some waves wash peacefully onto the sand and recede. Other waves crash, shaking the beach. Some waves wash far up on the sand, eroding sandcastles and foaming around the feet of unsuspecting sunbathers. One can sometimes look out on the horizon, see a very large swell approaching, and think, "I wonder if I should move the beach blanket—looks like the tide is coming in." *Cosmic Trends* will help you to protect your sandcastle and know when to move the beach blanket.

Yet this book is much more than a collection of astrological forecasts. It will empower you to see the future. However, this insight requires more than knowledge of the planets and signs. It takes something we each possess, but may not have developed—the part of our consciousness that can make connections and find similarities. We need to exercise the side of our brain that can see beneath the surface of events and, using the tools of astrology, make hidden connections. As you come to understand the meanings of the planets and signs in terms of the outer world, this book will give you opportunities to practice using this intuitive awareness. *Cosmic Trends* will include questions and interactive exercises—called Astro-Connections Activities and located at the ends of chapters—to help you apply the planets and signs to a world where so much seems random and unpredictable.

Part of the aim of this book is to present the myriad parts of our world that can be viewed and forecast through the lens of astrology. As you read these pages, allow yourself to enjoy observing all facets of modern culture. We can pick and choose the clothes we wear, but that does not mean everyone has to share our tastes. From the sublime to the ridiculous, from the spiritual to the profane, there is room for everyone. As Friar Laurence says in *Romeo and Juliet*, "the world is broad and wide."[2] We live more and more in a multicultural society and a cross-border world, so the planets' influences extend well beyond what many people think of when they think of culture. The outer planets affect everything—from the streets, thrift shops, and urban dance clubs to high couture and fine art museums.

Henry David Thoreau wrote: "If a man does not keep pace with his companions, perhaps it is because he hears a different drummer."[3] This book profiles a number of "different drummers" to illustrate qualities of the outer planets and zodiac signs. Some chapters will close with a profile of a famous person who embodies qualities of the planet or planetary pattern discussed in the chapter. This profile section is designed to help you see how the seemingly impersonal outer planets can spring to vibrant life in individuals, connecting people to important events and eras.

This book tries to present a balanced view of the future. In 1904, the St. Louis World's Fair celebrated a new century and the unfolding of a new world. The world's fair featured "palaces" that showcased advances in electricity, education, machinery, and manufacturing. It was an optimistic extravaganza, celebrating the new modern world. Much of the futurist literature of the time was similarly hopeful. Who would have guessed that the next forty years would feature two brutal world wars, Communist revolutions, and a reshaping of the world? Although many wonderful and helpful inventions came to pass during the twentieth century, it was a mistake to see the future through rose-colored glasses.

Interspersed throughout the book are brief Astrology Background boxes, intended to present astrology in more depth. These Astrology Background sections sometimes include detailed forecasts and horoscopes. Although some knowledge of astrology is necessary to read the Astrology Background boxes, most of *Cosmic Trends* can be read by those who are unfamiliar with how to read a horoscope.

This book is divided into four parts. Part I explains the influence of Pluto and how it affects generations. Part II is about major Pluto-influenced trends we will soon begin experiencing. Starting in 2008, Pluto's entry into Capricorn will rock our world in ways large and small. Part III is about present and future trends associated with Uranus and Neptune. Part IV is about some of the long-term planetary cycles that are at work deep within the culture.

Endnotes

1. Information Overload Statistics, Humboldt State University Library, http://library.humboldt.edu/~ccm/fingertips/ioverloadstats.html (accessed 22 August 2006).
2. William Shakespeare, *The Tragedy of Romeo and Juliet* (New York: Washington Square Press, 1992), 141.
3. Henry David Thoreau, *Walden and Other Writings,* ed. Brooks Atkinson (New York: The Modern Library, 1992), 305.

PART I

Connecting with Pluto

CHAPTER 1

Transformational Pluto

PLUTO IS . . .

Powerful
Intense
Obsessive
Exposing
Transforming
Extreme
Resourceful
Probing
Secretive

Pluto Background

Pluto does not rush through the zodiac. It takes its time—248 years to travel once around the sun, and anywhere from twelve to more than thirty years in each sign, depending on Pluto's distance from the sun. Although it takes its time making an impact, Pluto is determined to be felt, seen, and heard.

Although new discoveries have expanded the boundaries of our solar system, Pluto continues to be felt, seen, heard—and experienced. Traveling slowly through a zodiac sign, it brings to the surface the characteristics of that sign, making them visible in trends and world events.

Pluto is neither upbeat nor rosy. It tends to be a bit dark. Because Pluto moves so slowly and has rather overpowering tendencies, it is often associated with climactic historical events that take time to build momentum. These powerful forces often have their roots deep in the collective unconscious.

In astrology, each sign of the zodiac has a ruler (see Appendix C—Connecting with the Zodiac Signs). Pluto is the modern ruler of Scorpio. Before the discovery of Pluto in 1930, Scorpio's ruler had always been Mars. Pluto and Scorpio have much in common, however, so it seemed natural to assign rulership of Scorpio—the watery sign of secret, hidden depths—to Pluto, which courses through the cold and distant reaches of our solar system.

This chapter will look at the major ways Pluto influences our world.

- Pluto intensifies and magnifies qualities of the astrological sign through which it is traveling. The look and feel of a cultural era are influenced by Pluto, elevating facets of a zodiac sign to a visible extreme.
- Pluto represents the cyclic transformation of society and culture: death and rebirth, destruction and rebuilding.
- Pluto exposes the darkness. It brings the hidden to the surface. Pluto has the power to dredge up concealed secrets of modern culture.
- Pluto has to do with powerful forces in the world.

We don't think of Pluto as having much influence over store displays, best-seller lists, the size of blueberry muffins, or popular colors for automobiles. However, Pluto's influence is widespread. Its orbit encompasses the others. Pluto *intensifies* the sign it's in, so we get extra Libra or Scorpio or Sagittarius, depending on where Pluto is spending its time.

Pluto, God of the Underworld

The counters are stainless steel. The food workers wear uniforms and latex gloves. The tables, floors, and restrooms are cleaned and polished. The food preparation is quick and cheap. Each burger or taco is designed and assembled with remarkable precision and little variation. McDonald's founder Ray Kroc even conducted surprise inspections, paying special attention to restaurant cleanliness and the crispness of the French fries. Today, Americans spend more money on fast food than on higher education or new cars,[1] and three and a half million people are employed to prepare and serve countless ready-made meals for an on-the-go world.[2]

Then, in 2001, while Pluto was in Sagittarius, Eric Schlosser wrote a book titled *Fast Food Nation: The Dark Side of the American Meal,* which spent months atop the bestseller lists. *Fast Food Nation* fascinated readers with its behind-the-scenes look at the medical and social consequences of the modern fast food industry. Behind the shiny service counters was a brutal meat processing industry and a workforce devoid of the entrepreneurial individualism that gave rise to fast food's business successes in the first place. And for the first time, our fast food culture was seen as contributing to epidemics of obesity and diabetes.

Sagittarius has to do with expansion—including waist sizes, calorie content, and sales volume. Pluto reveals what's beneath the slick surface, in the dark recesses of the kitchens where breakfast sausages are made. It brings deep cultural secrets into the light of day. Like an exposé that reveals what has been happening behind the scenes, Pluto has the power to change our world by getting us to see the familiar in new and discomforting ways. Although small, dark, and distant, Pluto can have large, illuminating, and long-term effects.

Whether in the area of fast food, religion, or sports, Pluto reveals the darker side. As a society or culture, we begin to see a threat that was right under our noses, a threat we had failed to notice. Or that we just didn't *want* to see. Pluto provides the moment, the intersection of a growing collective willingness to confront the unseen monster.

Pluto is the God of the Underworld, so we often confront a facet of humanity's "heart of darkness," which manifests as the more extreme, unsavory elements of the zodiac sign through which Pluto is journeying. Pluto exposes what is happening when the soil is turned over and a nation, a culture, or a world sees something crawling in the moist loam, sees it for the first time. An initial shock, a jolt, is followed by a collective decision on a course of action.

An example is the 1997 death of Princess Diana, an event that took place not long after Pluto entered Sagittarius, often considered a sign of royalty. Her death shocked the world, causing a public re-examination of the meaning of the modern British monarchy, the cult of celebrity, marriage, and privacy.

Another way to think about Pluto is as a big plow, proceeding down the field of culture and society, turning over the earth so that the land can be reseeded. While this process might be advantageous for growing new crops, it can be a problem if you've built a nest in the field. The Scottish poet Robert Burns wrote, in "To a Mouse," about just such a field mouse. The mouse, seeing that winter was fast approaching, gathered nuts and seeds, and built a warm, secure nest in the field. The field mouse was prepared. But then the field was plowed under, and the mouse's nest was destroyed. The poet concludes that

The best-laid schemes o' mice an' men
Go oft awry,
An' leave us nought but grief an' pain,
For promis'd joy![3]

Like the unfeeling plow, Pluto turns over the soil. It need not, however, bring us the same grief and pain as was visited on the field mouse. In fact, maybe the field mouse will be inspired to move to a better field or to build a new nest out of harm's way. A lesson learned, a new awakening, or a renewal of purpose are all positive expressions of Pluto. However, history is filled with instances when the steel wedge of the plow was stronger than the field mouse.

Although Pluto represents death, death need not be physical. The soil being turned over by Pluto's plow can represent popular ideas or ideals. National or global illusions often die, depending on which sign Pluto is traveling through.

Pluto is also rebirth into a new form. It prepares the soil for new seeds. If the plow never renewed the topsoil, growing new crops would be difficult. Despite its seeming darkness and inconvenient exposing of secrets, Pluto symbolizes our survival and our ability to regenerate ourselves. When Pluto moves on, we can look around and see the sunlight streaming through the open windows of a transformed world.

Pluto: A Powerful Force

Pluto can act on our lives like a big freeway traffic jam or multi-car accident, producing in us a feeling of helplessness as we search for relief. The orange cones tell us to slow down, merge right or left, detour. Big flashing signs warn us to reduce our speed. The traffic slows to a crawl and we mutter about being late for work. Stuck in the same traffic snarl, we each cope in our own way: Taurus pops in a CD of soft music; Virgo turns the radio dial, looking for a traffic report; and Gemini picks up the cell phone.

There can be any number of reasons for a traffic jam. The road is old, worn, and potholed and needs to be replaced. Or a gasoline tanker truck has overturned, bursting into flames, and the freeway is closed—cars are being taken off at the exit and drivers are forced to navigate in unfamiliar territory.

Pluto is one of those freeway traffic jams that goes on for hours. We are moving in the same direction together, as a community or as a nation, when we suddenly come to a screeching halt and have to detour. When the way forward is blocked, drivers will even place their vehicles into reverse gear and try to navigate backwards to an exit just behind them.

Looking Within for Answers

There is another way of looking at this analogy, however. Who bears responsibility for the commuters' nightmare of an unanticipated traffic jam? Is it the construction workers who set up the orange cones? Is it the thoughtless bureaucracy that scheduled a massive repair project during the morning rush hour? Is it the truck driver who lost control of his vehicle? Or is it us, stuck in traffic and fuming over the wasted minutes of our lives? Looked at in another way, our personal dependence on automobiles has helped create the problem in the first place.

This is not intended to make us feel guilty about driving to work, but rather to illustrate how Pluto operates. Pluto re-routes our lives in ways that are often uncomfortable. Rather than project blame onto others, though, Pluto opens up the opportunity for shared self-examination. In fact, the everyday occurrence of freeway traffic jams has led to the slow development over the past few decades of more efficient mass transit. Pluto can help us, as a society or nation, to rethink our lives, looking for a better way.

Pluto Profile: Bob Dylan

Pluto can intensify an era. If you wanted to hear the future in 1961, when Pluto was in modest Virgo, you could have taken a good look around. Some people were already there—at Gerde's Folk City in Greenwich Village in New York City, to be exact. That's where the future was performing, wearing blue jeans and a proletarian Dutch Boy cap. Although he sang in a raspy voice and lacked stage polish, this innocuous poet/songwriter was soon to become the towering musical voice of a generation.

Bob Dylan's music was born out of the artistic moral conscience and folk music roots evident in Pluto's passage through Virgo. He was a product of his time and reflected the values and culture of a particular era just as much as he helped to shape those values.

When Pluto was in Virgo in the 1960s, the cultural icons of that decade embodied Virgo qualities. Virgo is associated with the harvest, folk dancing (those who are old enough may recall the 1960s folk dance craze inspired by *Zorba the Greek*), and music that springs out of communal sharing of the land. Folk music became mainstream when Pluto went into Virgo, and folk roots were evident in much of the popular music of the 1960s.

Bob Dylan writes in his autobiographical memoir *Chronicles* about his one-pointed obsession with folk music:

> *Folk music was all I needed to exist. Trouble was, there wasn't enough of it. It was out of date, had no proper connection to . . . the trends of the time. Once I'd slipped in beyond the fringes it was like my six-string guitar became a crystal magic wand and I could move things like never before. I had no other cares or interests besides folk music.*[4]

Bob Dylan was a musician who voiced a youthful folk ethos just as it surfaced in the culture. He was like a merman riding a hunchback whale as it breached the surface of the ocean. Pluto, which brought folk music to the surface when it moved into the sign of Virgo, found the perfect instrument in Bob Dylan.

Bob Dylan: Astrology Background

Bob Dylan has four planets—the Moon, Jupiter, Saturn, and Uranus—spread across the sign of Taurus. These four Taurus planets sextile Mercury in the horoscope for the United States and trine the U.S. Pluto, helping to give Dylan the hip corona that elevated him from ordinary to icon. Dylan's close natal conjunction of the Moon and Saturn showed in a 2004 interview he did on *60 Minutes*.[5] During the course of the interview, Dylan expressed a muted, even pessimistic, view of his fame and fortune.

When Dylan moved from his native Minnesota to New York in 1961 to begin his music career, Pluto was in the early degrees of Virgo. At that time, it squared his Gemini Sun while opposing his unassuming Pisces Mars.[6] As Dylan's fame accelerated, Pluto crossed over his Virgo Midheaven.

A Piscean Mars can also impart dreaminess. Dylan's autobiographical memoir *Chronicles*—published just as Pluto crossed over Dylan's natal Ascendant—clearly shows that Dylan saw his life and environment in New York as a kind of poetic dream state. Not surprisingly, given so much mutability—with

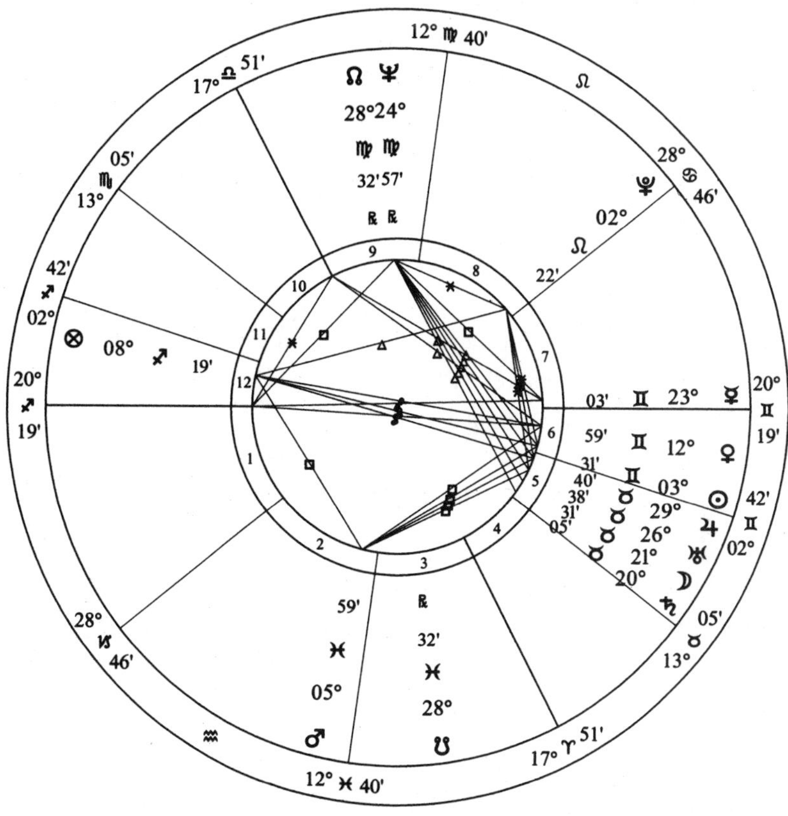

Bob Dylan
May 24, 1941 / 9:05 PM CST
Duluth, Minnesota / Placidus houses

five planets, the Ascendant, and Midheaven all in mutable signs and transiting Pluto, activating several of these in the 1960s—he changed his last name from Zimmerman to Dylan. He labored over this name change, parsing the connotative differences between "Allyn" and "Dylan."[7] In the 1960s, the temporary T-square formed by transiting Pluto brought this symbol of transformational change fully into Dylan's creative imagination. The focal point where this energy sought release was the Part of Fortune in his Twelfth House. As Pluto continued to move through Virgo, it separated from his Sun and squared his musical Gemini Venus.

Astro-Connections Activity

Astro-Poem

To make connections between the outer planets and trends you see in the world, it's helpful to develop the right side of the brain, the side of the brain that is more intuitive and able to synthesize. Simple creative writing exercises involving the planets can loosen up the right side of the brain and help break down the mental barriers between you and the energies of the planets and signs. To spot the planets at work in our world, it helps to know what those planets might "feel" or what they might say if they could talk—because in a way, they are speaking to us all the time through fashion trends, popular entertainment, and the latest car models.

The Astro-Poem is simple. Select a keyword for Pluto (see the keywords list on page 3) and write the poem. Throughout the poem, focus on trying to make connections with the keyword. Each line of the poem begins with two or three words, which are provided. Later, when you have read further in this book, you can return to the Astro-Poem for other outer planets.

I've written the first few lines below as an example, using a keyword for Pluto, so you can see how it might look. Keep the lines short, adding just two or three words. This exercise will bring out unexpected observations and connections.

I feel (planet or sign keyword).
*I wish for*_______________________,
*but discover*_______________________.
*I imagine*_______________________,
*but neglect*_______________________.
*I seek*_______________________,
*but find*_______________________.
*I understand*_______________________,
*but forget*_______________________.
*I love*_______________________,
*but need*_______________________.
*I weep for*_______________________,
*but dream*_______________________.
I feel (repeat keyword).

Sample Astro-Poem

I feel *extreme.*
I wish for *the end,*
but discover *a path.*
I imagine *loud sirens,*
but neglect *soft raindrops.*
I seek *to go faster,*
but find *I am breathless.*
I understand *pain,*
but forget *to heal.*
I love __________________ ,
but need ________________ .
I weep for ________________ ,
but dream ________________ .
I feel *extreme.*

Endnotes

1. Eric Schlosser, *Fast Food Nation: The Dark Side of the All-American Meal* (New York: Perennial, 2002), 3.
2. Schlosser, 6.
3. Robert Burns, "To a Mouse," *The Norton Anthology of English Literature: Fifth Edition,* ed. M. H. Abrams (New York: W.W. Norton & Company), 91–92.
4. Bob Dylan, *Chronicles: Volume One* (New York: Simon & Schuster, 2004), 236.
5. Bob Dylan, interview, "Dylan Looks Back," *60 Minutes,* CBS Television, 5 December 2004.
6. Ronald C. Davison uses this word—"unassuming"—to describe Mars in Pisces in *Astrology: The Classic Guide to Understanding Your Horoscope* (Sebastopol, California: CRCS Publications, 1979), 60.
7. Dylan, *Chronicles*, 78.

Chapter 2

Six Generations of Pluto, 1912–2008

Note: Refer to Appendix C for basic descriptions of the twelve zodiac signs and how they apply to our modern world.

One of the best ways to understand how Pluto influences cultural trends is to look at how it affects generations.

When Pluto goes through signs of the zodiac, it brings to the surface certain traits for each generation. Pluto puts its stamp on an era, and each generation of Pluto carries the imprint of that sign for a lifetime. The cross-influences of Pluto eras and Pluto generations help shape history, major trends, and current events.

By looking at recent past and present Pluto generations, we can get a clearer picture of how future trends will develop. The sign through which Pluto passes does not make us into predestined generational robots. It is rather a symbol of how each generation might interact with and shape the forces of history and world events. The interaction of generations and history forever binds us to one another, for better or for worse, and shapes broad changes in culture. The following descriptions of each Pluto generation explain some of the defining events and cultural trends of the time, and look at how people in each generation have manifested those traits as they've grown older.

Many of the Plutonian forces that reshape nations come from deep inside society and are not forced from outside. The hierarchical view of history—a top-down notion that we are mostly helpless pawns who act in accordance with historical forces and leaders beyond our control—has in recent years been challenged by the bottom-up theory that people can generate their own historical choices and consequent destiny. An upended hierarchy, where change is generated from the base of the pyramid, rather than dictated from the top, is one of the defining trends of the past century. Pluto is often the force of history manifesting from the bottom up.

A Generation Is . . .

A generation is a group of contemporaries who are shaped by similar cultural, social, and historical experiences. There are no strict rules for the age range within a generation. History shapes each generation's outline and boundaries. The shared experiences of youth contribute to generational bonding. Pluto in Leo Baby Boomers who have never met share a youthful common ground: musical icons, TV shows, or the assassination of President Kennedy. Similarly, an older generation grew up sharing the experience of the Great Depression and World War II. Anyone who has witnessed the Pluto in Cancer generation's graceful ballroom dancing becomes immediately aware of the unique generational bonds established through shared dance and music.

The Pluto in Cancer Generation

Pluto was in Cancer during the following time periods:

September 10, 1912–October 20, 1912
July 9, 1913–December 28, 1913
May 26, 1914–October 7, 1937
November 25, 1937–August 3, 1938
February 7, 1939–June 14, 1939

The Pluto in Cancer generation struggled through the Great Depression, fought fear, won a cataclysmic world war, and saved democracy. It is worth paying careful attention to what happened during Pluto's passage through Cancer because, in 2008, Pluto will enter Capricorn—Cancer's opposite sign in the zodiac. In astrology, opposite signs are powerfully linked, and the world-shaping forces that were active during Pluto's passage through Cancer will be re-awakened and challenged by new realities.

Cancer is ruled by the Moon, which gives rise to tidal changes; the power of water to shape the world is profound. John Dos Passos, in the novel *1919*—part of his *U.S.A.* trilogy—featured a sailor who was a pawn of world events, thrown hither and yon despite his own best efforts to exert some control over his life. Pluto again entered a water sign—Scorpio—in 1984, and the Pluto in

Scorpio generation (discussed in detail later in this chapter) is just now beginning to step into the adult world.

Every action gives rise to an opposing reaction. The opposition generated by Pluto's passage through a zodiac sign is signified by that sign's opposite. In the case of Cancer, its opposite sign in the zodiac is Capricorn, the sign of big business. When Pluto was in Cancer, there was a reaction against the concentration of money in the hands of a few. More power—Pluto represents power—was demanded by workers who felt the pain of economic dislocation. The Moon traditionally rules the people of a nation so, while Pluto was in Cancer, workers' trade unions formed and strengthened.

The sign of Cancer is the crab, protected by a shell and pincers. Cancer relates to home, country, and security; it is also associated with the bottommost point of the zodiac: our nurturing roots, our heritage. Many who were born while Pluto was in Cancer have spent countless satisfying hours exploring the leaves and branches of their family trees; they study geneaolgy because it is a family's roots. The search for roots can manifest—when present in a whole generation—as a desire to find that which connects us socially and culturally. Alex Haley, another member of the Pluto in Cancer generation, wrote the best-selling book *Roots* about his search for his African heritage. His book inspired many African-Americans with a sense of a uniquely shared historical identity.

Community and national identities are very important to Pluto in Cancer individuals. As a result, many are very patriotic. This was the last generation to exhibit an unbounded civic spirit through participation in a broad range of shared community activities, the result of generational bonding caused by the Great Depression and World War II.[1]

Pluto in Cancer values conformity in the positive sense of seeking unity rather than division. The Pluto in Cancer workforce placed a high premium on following the company line. IBM, a quintessential Pluto in Cancer corporation, was founded in 1924. It has traditionally fostered a buttoned-down business suit culture. In contrast, a company founded by Pluto in Leo innovators, Apple Computer, prides itself on its corporate culture of individualism.

"Cookie cutter" homes became available to Pluto in Cancer parents of young Pluto in Leo children as the suburbs grew after World War II. Conformity allows for the mass production and marketing of consumer goods, which took off starting with factory production of the Ford Model T in 1919.

The Pluto in Leo Generation

Pluto was in Leo during the following time periods:

October 7, 1937–November 25, 1937
August 3, 1938–February 7, 1939
June 14, 1939–October 20, 1956
January 15, 1957–August 19, 1957
April 11, 1958–June 10, 1958

Pluto rules the issues of psychological power and brings hidden things to light. Leo is the sign of the lion—the strong, paternal, charismatic leader. During the years that Pluto was in the sign of Leo, the world witnessed the effects of charismatic dictators and the subsequent bringing to light of the horrific results of dictatorial power.

When the bombs stopped falling at the end of World War II, the arrow on the birthrate chart began to shoot upward. Most demographers mark 1946 as the start of the Baby Boom, with a decline in the birth rate starting after 1957. However, the birthrate actually began to climb from 1940 to 1943, was interrupted for two years, then resumed its upward demographic trajectory in 1946. The Baby Boom generation, if it only included the post-World War II years, would have to exclude Bob Dylan (born in 1941), as well as John Lennon (1940) and Mick Jagger (1943). Pluto was in Leo from 1939 until 1958, and the earlier time span helps to account for the strong generational bonding many Baby Boomers felt, and continue to feel, for these musicians.

The generation born during this time wants to shine, and they have felt the inner fires burning for a lifetime. The beloved stars and movie directors of the Pluto in Leo generation—Tom Hanks, Goldie Hawn, and Steven Spielberg, to name just a few—captured and projected a childlike innocence. Entertainment and creative self-expression are keys to Leo in modern culture. The Pluto in Leo generation exhibits strong individualism, and they hold the power of an individual's personal creative expression in high esteem. Elvis Presley, "the King," became famous during Pluto's passage through Leo.

This generation has spent a great deal of time basking in the sun around a fountain of youth. Keeping up a youthful appearance for a lifetime is important to Pluto in Leos. Health clubs proliferated during the 1980s as Pluto in Leo young people began to look for ways to shape up and stay fit. Cosmetic surgery is achieving unprecedented growth as this generation begins to experience the wrinkles of age, and never have so many hair restoration remedies been promoted on late-night television infomercials.

Finding the inner child became one of the many quests embarked upon by this generation, who then became their own children's pals. Pluto in Leo is the child in the adult—or the adult child. There has been something a bit charming in the common sight of Pluto in Leo mothers who take as much delight in Barbie dolls as their daughters and Pluto in Leo fathers who still collect sports trading cards along with their sons. This is also the generation that has turned youth sports into a quasi-professional pressure cooker.

Leo is the romantic sign. Leos savor the flower-bouquet and love-note part of a relationship more than anything that follows. In fact, a number of Pluto in Leo spouses and partners have found that a key to relationship survival is constant courting. Dating services, now a popular online destination, first became popular during the 1970s and 1980s as the Pluto in Leo generation hit their twenties and thirties. Personal newspaper ads began to blossom in local weeklies as this generation of young lions and lionesses warily circled one another, looking for that heartthrob of true jungle love.

Leo is a gambler. They are the risk takers of the zodiac. President Bill Clinton is a Leo who exuded a sunny, optimistic charisma. He also gambled in his dalliance with a White House intern, risking his presidency in the process. Leo does not think long and hard about consequences. The lion pounces. The result can be a warm and sheltering embrace, captured prey, or a leap into the unknown with no idea what might strike the lion's exposed chest in midflight. The lion lives for that moment of opportunity when great reward and crashing fall intersect.

Leo is idealistic, some might even say unrealistic. It loves to entertain and be loved. This is the generation that sees the world through rose-colored glasses.

The Pluto in Virgo Generation

Pluto was in Virgo during the following time periods:

October 20, 1956–January 15, 1957
August 19, 1957–April 11, 1958
June 10, 1958–October 5, 1971
April 17, 1972–July 30, 1972

Pluto's passage through Virgo marked the era of large engineering organizations, such as NASA and Xerox, built on teamwork. This time period saw the space program's greatest accomplishments. Apollo 13, launched in 1970 and crippled in flight, was later celebrated in the movie of the same name. Engineers with crew cuts, white shirts, and slide rules saved the mission. Those who have seen the movie *Apollo 13* may recall the scene in which a team of NASA engineers successfully worked with methodical, no-nonsense, can-do creativity within a strict time limit in order to fashion a life-saving adapter from random scraps of material available on the space module. Engineers were heroes.

Pluto in Virgo saw a shift towards greater health awareness. Health food stores, organic food, and yoga began their long ascent into the cultural mainstream when Pluto was in Virgo. The Pluto in Leo youth who came of age during Pluto in Virgo applied their leonine self-absorption to the pursuit of natural health. The macrobiotic brown rice diet was popular, and land-based communes were a Virgo phenomenon.

Virgo is a mutable sign, meaning it is associated with rapid change (Sagittarius, Pluto's present location until 2008, is also a mutable sign). Bob Dylan's early anthem was "The Times They Are a-Changin'." The Beatles, although they were very much a Neptune in Scorpio music phenomenon (discussed in more detail in chapter 8), also had qualities associated with Pluto's passage through Virgo. They were mutable, experiencing rapid musical change. They rose to popularity wearing nice suits and boyish mod haircuts, giving them a somewhat ambisexual aura. They had amazing technical virtuosity, and their albums were increasingly products of recording-studio engineering advancements. The Beatles were attentive to detail. They easily reflected what was happening in society, an association of Virgo with the reflective sign it opposes, Pisces.

Many of the robotic developments in medical surgery are driven by Pluto in Virgo doctors and researchers who are now hitting their peak of professional accomplishment. Meticulous Pluto in Virgo engineers are also bringing new designs to theme park thrill rides.

Although Apple Computer was started by two visionary Pluto in Leo computer whizzes, its technical operating-system wizardry was designed by Pluto in Virgo software engineers. Apple's Macintosh computers are widely used today in editing and graphic design, two areas in which Virgo excels. Speaking of wizardry, *Harry Potter* author J. K. Rowling is a Pluto in Virgo.

Pluto in Virgo actors and actresses are usually not stars in the same way as Pluto in Leo performers. They strive above all for meticulous honesty and integrity. Pluto in Virgo actor Sean Penn, for instance, excels at blending into a role, losing himself in a character. He does not have a Pluto in Leo celebrity persona that shines through in each role he plays. Pluto in Virgo actress Renée Zellweger also blends into whatever character she is portraying in a movie, surrendering her own identity. Johnny Depp, another Pluto in Virgo performer, has made a career out of playing idiosyncratic, diverse characters in movies such as the *Pirates of the Caribbean* series and *Finding Neverland.*

Virgo is often thought of as a sign of conformity, of trying to fit into the organization and serve the greater whole. However, it is an earth sign associated with the harvest season and so there is a pagan element to the sign that can manifest as rebellion against over-civilized social norms and mores. Pluto in Virgo can bring out the dark rebel in a culture. It is also a sign that needs to find meaning in life beyond everyday material necessities.[2] Kurt Cobain, singer and songwriter for the band Nirvana, was born with Pluto in Virgo.

Pluto in Virgo brings out the power of the feminine. Several Pluto in Virgo singer-songwriters have helped to give women more power in music. Sarah McLachlan has had a number of hit songs and also founded the Lilith Fair, a touring concert series featuring female singers and rock groups. Tori Amos has explored deep Plutonian emotions in her songs. Melissa Etheridge is a concert rock star who is married to a woman and speaks out for gay rights.

Television shows often personify broad transformations in culture. Several Pluto in Virgo television shows, such as *I Dream of Jeannie* and *Bewitched*, portrayed the gathering release of feminine power as well as male attempts to keep it under control.

The Pluto in Libra Generation

Pluto was in Libra during the following time periods:

October 5, 1971–April 17, 1972
July 30, 1972–November 5, 1983
May 18, 1984–August 28, 1984

Pluto in Libra is associated with the transformation of relationships. Divorce laws, gay rights and partnerships, and the feminist movement all gathered steam during Pluto's passage through Libra.

The divorce rate rose and spiked in the 1970s. By 1980, one out of every four marriages ended in divorce.[3] If the Pluto in Libra *Friends* generation is all about relationships, they are also a generation that suffered disproportionate Plutonian pain because of the upended relationships within their own families.

A popular movie of the 1970s was *Kramer vs. Kramer,* starring Dustin Hoffman and Meryl Streep as a married couple with a young son. Streep played a mother who departed on a mission of self-discovery, leaving behind a workaholic husband who had to learn to be a parent. The central conflict in the movie was framed as a court custody battle. The film touched a raw nerve in American society at the time of its release because it mirrored, as movies so often do, the Pluto in Libra cultural transformation then taking place.

Pluto entered Libra to stay in late July 1972. Just a little over a month before this momentous transition, there was a break-in at the Democratic National Committee offices in the Watergate Hotel complex, which precipitated the chain of events leading to President Richard Nixon's resignation. Watergate was like a slow-motion car wreck. Gradually, the orange cones—subpoenas, hearings, news-magazine cover stories—appeared. The nation slowed to a crawl as the news came to be dominated by stories of Watergate. The Watergate scandal and Nixon's resignation were, in a sense, a macro-divorce court where the custody of the nation was at stake. It was Pluto in Libra writ large.

American Graffiti, a movie that helped awaken 1950s nostalgia, debuted in the summer of 1973, shortly after Pluto entered Libra. The movie was released at about the same time that President Richard Nixon's Watergate tapes were discovered and subpoenaed. Nostalgia is one way of re-establishing Libran balance and harmony when the present has become too serious. *American Graffiti*—and Pluto in Libra—ushered in a wave of 1950s nostalgia, giving us *Happy Days,* the Fonz, *Laverne & Shirley,* and a chain of Mel's Drive-Ins.

Creative, artistic, and dreamy Neptune began to influence the Pluto in Libra generation starting in 1998 and will continue to exert a powerful influence until 2012. This planetary pattern shows that the childhood pain of the Pluto in Libra generation finds release through popular music and movie imagery. When the movie *Titanic* was released, audiences went for the cold iceberg and stayed for the hot romance. The doomed, transforming romance of Jack and Rose—played by an actor and actress both with Pluto in Libra—spoke to the hearts of a Pluto in Libra generation of former latchkey kids of divorced parents, and the movie tapped into a vast ocean current of longing for true love and redemptive meaning.

Pluto in Libra: Astrology Background

In 1998, Neptune moved into Aquarius and began to trine (a 120-degree angle) the oldest members of the Pluto in Libra generation. The trine is an angle that is warm and positive. It inspires a sense of well-being. The movie *Titanic* was released in December 1997—just one month before Neptune began to trine the Pluto in Libra generation. As the movie began to shatter all box office records, Neptune moved into Aquarius.

The blindfolded scales-of-justice generation will always weigh the truth of relationships everywhere, including the relationship between citizen and government. Punk rock group Green Day won a Grammy Award in 2005 for their hit album *American Idiot,* which has been described as a punk opera. All three members of this commercially vibrant band were born just as Pluto was entering Libra. One was born to a heroin-addicted mother who put him up for adoption; then he watched as his adoptive parents got divorced when he was seven years old. Another band member was raised by his widowed waitress mother after he lost his truck-driver father to cancer.[4] The title song of *American Idiot* is about a government that relates to its citizens through fear and alienation. The lyrics express a determination to go down a different, better path.

In the Iraq War, many of the junior field lieutenants are young Pluto in Libra soldiers. Growing up in the divorce culture of the 1970s, they learned self-reliance and survival skills. They also lack the usual decorum when it comes to respecting the military hierarchy. These proved to be battlefield assets when a number of these junior officers exhibited an adaptability and tactical brilliance that saved troops' lives and earned the grudging respect of commanding officers.[5] We can expect the Pluto in Libra generation to continue to be tough under fire, independent, and accustomed to taking care of themselves in all areas of civic life, not just on the battlefield.

The Pluto in Scorpio Generation

Pluto was in Scorpio during the following time periods:

November 5, 1983–May 18, 1984
August 28, 1984–January 17, 1995
April 21, 1995–November 10, 1995

Pluto's passage through the sign of Scorpio brought out the startling synergies between this sign and its planetary ruler.

Music associated with Pluto often expresses society's dark thoughts. If you wanted to see the future in 1990, it was wearing a flannel shirt, ripped jeans, and heavy black boots, while listening to music a grungy few might think of as Nirvana. More than a decade after the death of lead singer Kurt Cobain, this seminal Pluto in Scorpio band continues to be a defining influence in rock music, and their signature guitar sound—a grinding sonic rush of sludgy white noise—is now a standard rock music convention.

As Pluto plowed through dark, intense, emotional Scorpio, new twelve-step and self-help groups proliferated. Adult Children of Alcoholics, incest survivors, and others sought to help people turn over the soil of past childhood traumas and plant new seeds. One bumper sticker even read, "It's Never Too Late to Have a Happy Childhood."

Kurt Cobain of Nirvana: Astrology Background

The Uranus-Pluto conjunction straddled Kurt Cobain's Ascendant. Aside from this conjunction, all the other planets in his horoscope were in water signs. This gave his Uranus-Pluto conjunction added power. Since it was on his Ascendant, all the water in his chart flowed outward through this conjunction.

Those born while Pluto was in Scorpio are noted for their extreme intensity. A highly visible minority of this generation enjoys the caffeinated jolt of Red Bull energy drinks, likes to hear a pounding bass beat, and can swear up a blue streak. Trends are taken to an extreme, and in fact one of the keys discovered by advertisers for this generation of consumers is "ex"—as in Xbox or extreme sports.

The generation born while Pluto was in Scorpio has grown up shouldering an extraordinary load—literally. School backpacks are no longer used just for carrying notebooks and pens. They are packed with survival gear: water bottles, snacks, math calculators, and heavy books. Slouched and with knees buckling under the load, students today look like marines who have just landed in a combat zone.

These young people have also been assigned an extraordinary amount of homework. It is not unusual for students as young as eight or nine to labor over an assignment late into the evening or to endure days of rigorous testing. They are being prepared for the future—although that future may not be the one envisioned by adult planners and educators. One of the qualities of Scorpio—and the generation marked by Pluto's transit through the sign of the scorpion—is the ability to develop shared survival resources and harbor them for an uncertain future.

"Teepeeing" a house—draping the front lawn, bushes, and trees with fresh toilet paper in the dark of night, like mischievous Navy SEALs or Army Rangers—is considered by today's youth to be a badge of honor. Some youths even leave a polite note with the toilet paper, saying they will be back to clean it up in the morning. Without yet being aware of it, are they a generation preparing for a stealth mission?

Some of the Pluto in Scorpio generation enjoys wearing darkly menacing fashions,

Preparing for a Storm?

A fashion made popular by the Pluto in Scorpio generation is the dark knit ski cap. Having been raised in New England, I associate the ski cap with cold weather, darkness, and snow. The knit ski cap means hunkering down against the storm, hunching your shoulders, lowering your head, and letting the blizzard hit while trudging through the snow. One stretches the cap down over the ears to keep out the biting wind. Having seen too many B-movies, I also associate the dark knit ski cap with a menacing dark-alley presence. Like the ski cap, both Pluto and Scorpio know how to survive a strong storm. The snow has not yet started falling on this generation, but they are already protecting their heads.

Doc Martens, and freaky white scrawls on black cotton sweatshirts. They helped to popularize gothic fashions. The Pluto in Scorpio generation even has its own day, Día de los Muertos. The Day of the Dead is growing in popularity in the U.S. and getting bigger every year—it's Halloween stripped, without the apple-bobbing and good-fairy costumes.

Pluto is about exposing and transforming. Scorpio is secret depths and hidden emotions. Home makeover shows have flourished in the wake of the events of September 11, 2001, as people turn to their homes for warmth and security. These television shows are especially popular with young Pluto in Scorpio viewers,[6] which might seem curious because most of these young people do not own their own homes. However, the shows bring added emotional depth and resonance—characteristics of Scorpio—to home decorating and remodeling. They make heartwarming sagas out of home remodeling, investing the process with a tearful joy.

There are several variations of this TV-show format, but the basic premise is that transforming a home is somewhat equivalent to transforming a life. In *Extreme Makeover: Home Edition,* a team of contractors, carpenters, designers, and interior decorators rebuilds a home for a family in need of a makeover. Right now, it is a home makeover on television. Later, it will be larger parts of society and the world that will get a makeover. This trend will be played out in many forms and variations over the next fifty years as the Pluto in Scorpio generation matures, ages, and takes control. The key will always be extreme transformation. The home is not simply patched and remodeled. It is completely torn down and a new one constructed in its place with the expectation that this is somehow tied to a personal, inner transformation on the part of the residents.

"Extreme" is a commercial buzzword that appeals directly to Pluto in Scorpio. In addition to *Extreme Makeover: Home Edition,* TV also presently offers *Extreme Makeover* (with transforming cosmetics and clothing), *Extreme Machines,* and *Extreme Cuisine.*

The Pluto in Scorpio generation is beginning to lead us deep into a mythical place in the national psyche. They have helped to popularize modern country-pop music, taking young listeners to an imaginary age when guys loved their dads, women could be proud carousers, and whiskey lullabies were sung for soldiers back home from a war.

Pluto Profile: Avril Lavigne

Avril Lavigne is one of a new wave of Pluto in Scorpio musical artists. She was born in Canada in 1984, just after Pluto moved into the sign of the scorpion. She has a powerful alignment of planets in Scorpio, giving this sign a great deal of power in her music.

Let Go, her first album, was released when she was just seventeen, and it catapulted her into stardom. Songs like "Complicated" and "Sk8er Boi" projected teen girl power. The album sold over fourteen million copies and received eight Grammy nominations.

In her music, Avril Lavigne embodies many of the qualities of Pluto:

- "Complicated" is about exposing what's under the surface of a person, seeing what's real.
- "Sk8er Boi" is written from the point of view of a girl who ended up with the punk skater that other girls rejected because of peer pressure. The catch is that the punk skater is now a music superstar on MTV and the girl who saw beneath the surface is now sharing his glory and writing his songs, including ostensibly this one. It's a revenge song, perfect for a singer with lots of stingers in her horoscope.
- The title of Lavigne's second CD, *Under My Skin,* could easily be a metaphor for the exposing, probing, and transforming power of Pluto. "Don't Tell Me," the hit song from that CD, flat out tells guys to back off. She doesn't give in or up, and she is defiantly not a boy toy. In concert, Lavigne introduces "Don't Tell Me" by telling girls to stay strong.

Avril Lavigne: Astrology Background

With four planets in Scorpio, this singer strives for authenticity and power. Avril Lavigne's Venus and Pluto are conjunct, giving her an uncanny ability to go beneath the surface with music. Her birth time is not known, but her Moon is most likely in Scorpio, adding to the dark intensity of her public image. She is a Libra Sun, always looking to balance the scales—especially in relationships.

The Pluto in Sagittarius Generation

Pluto was or will be in Sagittarius during the following time periods:

January 17, 1995–April 21, 1995
November 10, 1995–January 26, 2008
June 14, 2008–November 27, 2008

Sagittarius has to do with religion and spirit. One day after Pluto entered Sagittarius to stay in 1995, Joan Osborne's song "One of Us," which depicts God as a poorly dressed bus passenger, entered the Top Forty and went into heavy rotation on VH1. The song ended up providing the musical theme for the TV show *Joan of Arcadia*—which was about a teenager who communicated with God.

Pluto in Sagittarius has opened the door to a wave of spirituality in American culture. Looking at bestseller lists and browsing through bookstores are ways to get a clear feel for what is important in a culture. While Pluto traveled through Sagittarius, many bestsellers had to do with spirituality, religion—and wizardry. The first book in the *Harry Potter* series was published in Britain in 1997, a year after Pluto entered Sagittarius to stay. J. K. Rowling's series of seven *Harry Potter* books is expected to be completed shortly before Pluto leaves Sagittarius.

The Da Vinci Code is a best-selling novel about the secrets of the Catholic Church. *The Five People You Meet in Heaven* is another book with a strong spiritual theme: a carnival-ride mechanic dies and meets five people in the afterlife, all of whom impart life lessons. Rick Warren's *The Purpose-Driven Life* was adopted by many churches seeking to bolster their missions.

Sagittarius, ruled by Jupiter, also has to do with expansion. The effects of this transit are everywhere, from super-sized meals at McDonald's to super-sized vehicles such as the Hummer. We can find Pluto's Sagittarian influence from the Mars Rover to steroids to the caffeine content at Starbucks.

Sport utility vehicles are just one example of how Pluto in Sagittarius has brought an obsession with large sizes. Housing developments have sprouted "starter mansions," two-story tract homes with three-car garages and vaulted cathedral ceilings. While we sit in front of the TV and watch *others* work out on the basketball court or baseball field, obesity has become a national epidemic. Many athletes have been discovered to have increased their muscle size through performance-enhancing drugs such as steroids.

Sagittarius likes to eat well and enjoy the good life. The sign's ruling planet, Jupiter, enjoys a good feast. So it was no surprise when obesity became an issue while Pluto traveled through Sagittarius. Restaurant menus began sporting calorie counters, and low-carbohydrate foods surged in popularity. Once again, Pluto brought a hidden problem to the surface and society was forced to pay attention.

In addition to large sizes, Sagittarius is also associated with religion and sports. All three qualities of Sagittarius—size, sports, and religion—converge on the modern basketball court where godlike athletes soar in the air.

The combination of religious authority and sex has also been brought into the uncomfortable light of day. Sexual abuse by those in positions of church power has been exposed on a scale deemed unimaginable just a short decade earlier. Pluto in Sagittarius has brought strong, polarizing religious and ideological landmines. *The Passion of the Christ,* Mel Gibson's movie about the Crucifixion, was both worshipped and criticized.

Sagittarius can be a comic sign. Pluto, although not a great comic like Mercury or Jupiter, also displays a lighter side when in Jupiter-ruled Sagittarius. Comedian Lenny Bruce, who used humor to expose society's dark secrets, had a strong combination of Jupiter and Pluto in his horoscope.

Pluto in Sagittarius is symbolized by two explorations that have gone in opposite directions. While Pluto was in Sagittarius, unmanned space missions brought the planets to us in four-color close-up. The Hubble telescope, too, has shown

Pluto in Sagittarius at the Mall

When Pluto first entered Sagittarius in 1995, I was browsing through stores at an outdoor mall. One of these was a new store devoted to selling decorative objects lit with a black light—a barely visible light in the near-ultraviolet range. Black light works best in dark or near-dark surroundings where it appears dark purple and reflects off of bright fluorescent colors. The only light in the store was black light, suffusing the interior with a dark purple misty glow. The display floor was packed shoulder to shoulder with people who had stepped in off the street to gawk at the colorful twirling mobiles, bright opalescent tchotchkes, and black-light posters. It was happy and different. My first thought was, "Pluto in Sagittarius!" Sagittarius is a partying sign and this store was having a party.

Soon after, I began to notice a proliferation of wooden carts selling jewelry and trinkets at indoor and outdoor malls, reminding me of gypsy carts. Pluto entered Sagittarius, the sign of the gypsy (usually in the broader sense of an adaptable traveler on life's byways), just as we began to buy jewelry off of wooden carts to grace toes, nostrils, and belly buttons, making us look like gypsies. At the same time, henna, a cosmetic body art imported from India and used by gypsies, also became popular.

Car Generations

Automobiles have Pluto generations, too.

In 1886, Karl Benz patented the first internal combustion engine. A Plutonian invention, the internal gas ignites in a cylinder, driving a piston stroke. With such an engine at its symbolic nucleus, is it any wonder that the American automobile became a symbol of teenage backseat sexual liberation?

Pluto in Cancer—As Pluto entered the sign of Cancer in 1913-1914, Henry Ford was just instituting an assembly line for producing the black model T—the dominant car on the market at the time. Cancer is the sign of home and family, and while Pluto was in Cancer, the automobile became a member of the family. It even had its own room—the garage—in new homes. On Sundays, families drove for the sheer pleasure of the experience much like a teenager with a new driver's license. Cancer is the sign of the crab and, like crabs in protective steel shells, Americans ventured tentatively past the limiting margins of local communities, and out into the surrounding world.

Pluto in Leo—Leo the lion is a combustible fire sign. Look at cars from the Pluto in Leo 1940s. Listen to them in the movies of that era. Cars ruled. They were big and hump-shouldered like lions. They prowled the roads, warmly embracing their occupants, and were associated with escape and leisure. Some cars sported big fins—which were supposed to suggest the fire power of rockets.

continued . . .

us distant galaxies. At the same time, cyberspace has opened up before our eyes. What used to be called the information superhighway is now a vast new virtual world rapidly being populated with cities and towns and little out-of-the-way hamlets, as well as by lawless criminals and helpful guides.[7]

Pluto in Sagittarius is also responsible, along with several other astrological patterns that will be discussed later in this book, for the booming new world of cyberspace games. Online games have attracted millions to a virtual Sagittarian world of jousts and tournaments.

The Pluto in Capricorn Generation

Pluto will be in Capricorn during the following time periods:

January 26, 2008–June 14, 2008
November 27, 2008–March 23, 2023
June 11, 2023–January 21, 2024
September 1, 2024–November 20, 2024

This generation will be discussed in detail in Part II, "Connecting with the Future: Pluto in Capricorn."

Astro-Connections Activity

Astrology Journals

Keeping an astrology journal can help you reflect on your own life and the world around you. It can help you to see and understand the world through the lens of astrology in a thoughtful, independent, and personal way. Where do you see Pluto in the world around you, and what is it doing? Look at cars, architecture, popular fads, and write down what you see. After reading other parts of this book, you can make sense of the world through Uranus, Neptune, and major conjunctions by continuing to write journals that explore these connections.

Notice things around you without judgment. Pick one thing you notice and write about it. What does it say? Does it seem to have the energy of Pluto, Uranus, or Neptune? I did something like this when I discussed the fashion of the knit ski cap on page 23. I have reproduced the passage here to give you an idea about how to begin using a journal to make associations between the world, objects, people, and the symbols of astrology.

A fashion made popular by the Pluto in Scorpio generation is the dark knit ski cap. Having been raised in New England, I associate the ski cap with cold weather, darkness, and snow. The knit ski cap means hunkering down against the storm, hunching your shoulders, lowering your head, and letting the blizzard hit while trudging through the

Pluto in Virgo—Virgo is modest, unpretentious, and likes to serve. The Volkswagen Beetle found success in the American market when Pluto entered Virgo. It became one of the most popular vehicles on the road, serving the needs of a growing population seeking to squeeze a car into the family budget. Volkswagen sales increased until the late 1960s. One saw Volkswagens all over the road throughout the 1960s—much as one sees SUVs massed in parking lots today. In 1968, the Walt Disney Company released a movie about a talking Volkswagen named Herbie. When Pluto entered Libra, demand for the Beetle began to wane.

Pluto in Libra—Libra is the sign of relationships. When Pluto entered Libra, cars became friendly sidekicks on TV shows. Starsky and Hutch rushed to crime scenes in their red-and-white Ford Gran Torino. Bo and Luke on *The Dukes of Hazzard* clambered in and out of a Dodge Charger named the General Lee. In the 1980s TV show *Knight Rider*, a Pontiac Trans Am named KITT shared wisecracks with David Hasselhoff. The 1970s were also the golden age of that male sexual-relationship fantasy: the van, memorialized in Sammy Johns's song about free love in a Chevy van.

Pluto in Scorpio—One month after Pluto entered Scorpio, *Christine*—a horror movie based on a Stephen King novel about a possessed 1958 Plymouth Fury—was released. Cars went

continued . . .

from *The Dukes of Hazzard* to real hazards. *Terminator 2* exhibited a leather-clad Arnold Schwarzenegger atop a rumbling, menacing motorcycle.

Pluto in Sagittarius—In keeping with the symbolism of Sagittarius, Pluto's transit through this sign has indulged us with large-size sport utility vehicles and Humvees—also known as Hummers. The Volkswagen Beetle came back, but had taken steroids.

Pluto in Capricorn—The future of cars will be discussed in greater detail in chapter 12, but a few future car trends are worth mentioning here. Beginning in 2008, automobiles will feature nostalgic designs. Expect to see vehicles that look like bread trucks and surf wagons with side wood paneling. The retro-styled Mini Cooper continues to grow in popularity with additions like a black-and-white checkerboard roof to enhance its 1960s appeal. There will be a move to embrace past car designs instead of futuristic ones. Hybrid cars will continue to grow in popularity and reliability. Sport utility trucks—tough and practical SUVs with truck beds—will be among the most popular vehicles on the road. In keeping with Pluto's exit from Jupiter-ruled Sagittarius and entry into Saturn-ruled Capricorn, serious vehicle downsizing will take place. Cars will be designed to show up rather than to show off.

snow. One stretches the cap down over the ears to keep out the biting wind. Having seen too many B-movies, I also tend to associate the dark knit ski cap with a menacing dark-alley presence. Like the ski cap, both Pluto and Scorpio know how to survive a strong storm. The snow has not yet started falling on this generation, but they are already protecting their heads.

Here are some suggestions for your own planet journal topics, all of which tend to reflect larger changes in culture:

1. New and different headwear
2. Alternative fashions
3. Anything in the news that exposes hidden, secret problems
4. Popular books
5. A popular movie
6. A shift in language—new words, slang, or usage
7. A popular television show or a trend in television shows
8. Cars and trucks—size, styling, colors, trends
9. Popular music or a type of music that is popular, especially among young people
10. Foods—restaurants, fast foods, supermarkets (There are deep connections between food and culture.)

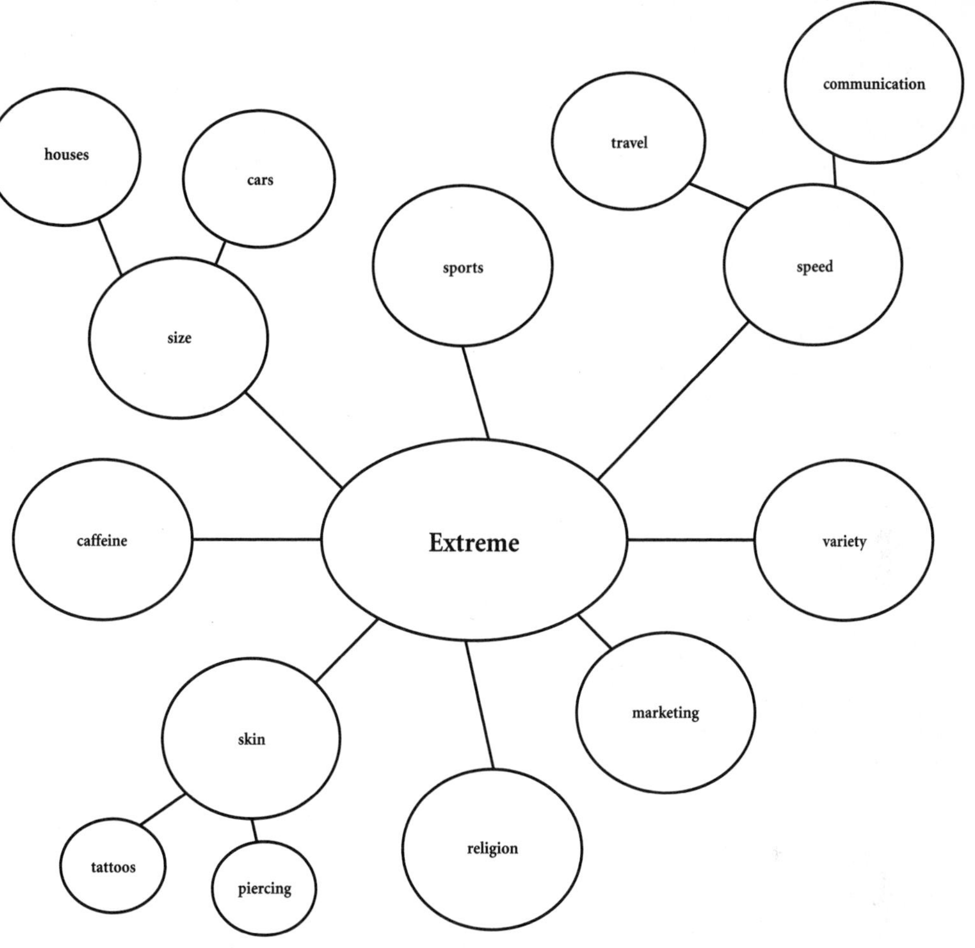

Astro-Connections Activity

Bubbles

For the central word in the middle of these bubbles, use one of the Pluto keywords from the chart on page 3. Free associate to come up with connections. Let your mind go. Not only will you find your right brain coming unstuck, but you will be able to make amazing connections between planets, signs, and our world. Don't inhibit yourself. I've done one for you and given you a blank web on the following page. Don't hesitate to add additional bubbles.

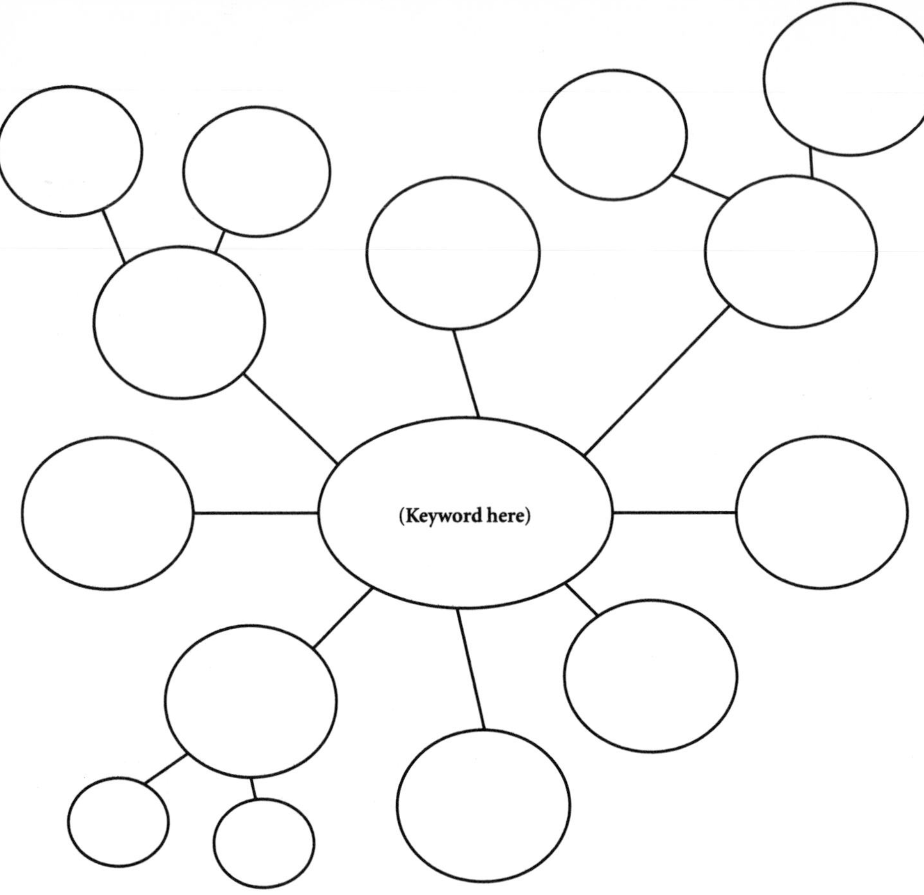

Endnotes

1. Robert A. Putnam, *Bowling Alone: The Collapse and Revival of American Community* (New York: Simon and Schuster, 2000), 267–272. Robert Putnam also shows how television and long work commutes have contributed to a decline in civic involvement.
2. Paul Wright, *Astrology in Action* (Sebastopol, California: CRCS Publications, 1989), 23.
3. National Center for Health Statistics: Advance report, Final Divorce Statistics, 1980. *Monthly Vital Statistics Report.* Vol. 32–No. 3, Supp, DHHS Pub. No. (PHS) 83–1, 120. Public Health Service, Hyattsville, Maryland, June 1983.
4. "Green Day: Biography," Artist Direct website, http://www.artistdirect.com/nad/music/artist/bio/0,,421234,00.html#bio (accessed 22 August 2006).
5. Dan Baum, "Battle Lessons," *The New Yorker*, 17 January 2005: 42–48.
6. According to primetime television ratings on http://www.allyourtv.com, *Extreme Makeover: Home Edition* was, in late 2005, the top-rated program among teenagers in its competitive time slot.
7. Steven Forrest, *The Book of Pluto* (San Diego, California: ACS Publications, 1994), 176. In this book, published a year before Pluto entered Sagittarius, the author predicted explorations of both outer space and cyberspace. Over ten years later, I have merely paraphrased and confirmed his forecasts.

PART II

Connecting with the Future: Pluto in Capricorn

When Pluto enters Capricorn in 2008, where it will stay until 2024, there will be a rending cultural jolt. Jupiter-ruled Sagittarius is all about expansion—exploring Mars, opening up the online world, travel, and adventure. Saturn-ruled Capricorn is all about limitations. That's not necessarily a bad thing, but it will be a rather shocking cultural contrast. There are some *similarities, though, and people will try to hold on to these similarities for dear life just because the familiar is secure.*

CHAPTER 3

Saturn, Capricorn's Security Planet

SATURN IS . . .

Laws

Maturity

Patience

Integrity

Stability

Limitation

Government

Aging

Security

Status Quo

Boundaries

Protection

Detachment

Saturn Background

On September 11, 2001, the security and stability of the United States came under attack. Two airplanes struck the World Trade Center, a third hit the Pentagon, and a fourth plane crashed in Pennsylvania before it could reach its terrorist target. At the time of these attacks, a powerful alignment of Saturn and Pluto was taking place. In 2008, Pluto will enter the sign of Capricorn, which is ruled by Saturn. Once again the astrological symbol of intensity and explosive transformation will be symbolically linked with the planet of structure, boundaries, and security.

Although this book pays particular attention to the outer planets—the ones beyond Saturn—Saturn will assume great importance because it rules Capricorn.

Saturn-Pluto: Astrology Background

Saturn and Pluto were in opposition from August 5, 2001, until May 25, 2002. This alignment, which occurs every thirty-three years on average, last took place in the mid-1960s.

Stressful aspects between Saturn and Pluto will develop in 2010 when they will be in a square aspect (90 degree angle) to one another. Our security will once again be affected. In astrology, oppositions and squares are casual links in a cyclic chain of events.

When it comes to earthly events and trends, Capricorn is one of the most important signs of the zodiac. It is often thought of as a low-key, hard-working, industrious goat in a black bow tie. However, as we shall see, Capricorn and its planetary ruler have a complexity that far exceeds this stereotype. Capricorn is both the heights and the depths. It is sometimes an office cubicle, sometimes a carnival, and sometimes it is like wooden Russian nesting dolls, one hiding inside another and another.

Capricorn is an earth sign, but its earthiness is different from the rich loam of Taurus or the neatly plowed corn rows of Virgo. Capricorn is associated with the hard and rocky mountaintop, the highest earthly plane. It is also the highest point in the natural horoscope, the gateway to heaven—making it, potentially, a very spiritual sign. One of the traits we can forecast for the coming Pluto in Capricorn era is a heightened spirituality attained as the result of hard knocks. Pluto in Capricorn spirituality will come about as a result of stumbling up difficult, rocky terrain into thin air.

The Tenth House: Astrology Background

In older, traditional astrology, which examined nations and rulers, the Tenth House was considered to be the most important and powerful of all the astrological houses. The Tenth House is the natural house of Capricorn, so in that sense Capricorn is a very important sign in the outer affairs of the world.

Key Characteristics

Saturn and Capricorn have several key characteristics in common, which will assume great importance when Pluto moves into the sign of Capricorn in 2008:

- Saturn and Capricorn both have to do with government and social control.
- Saturn, especially, is the fear of letting go and losing control.
- Saturn and Capricorn are both associated with down-to-earth, hard-headed practicality.
- They are both patient and persevering.

The Goatfish

Capricorn is a complex sign, half goat and half fish.

In classical myth, Capricorn is associated with the lusty goat god Pan, a satyr with the spindly legs and hooves of a goat who played a musical instrument known as the panpipes. Pan tried to escape from Typhon by leaping into a river. From Pan's escape, we get the word *panic*. Pan's dive into the river caused him to grow a fish's tail.[1] Capricorn is not just a goat. It's a goatfish. This shows the dual nature of the sign, striving for the heights while also attracted to the depths.[2]

Capricorn has several qualities related to its association with the goat. Capricorn can bring out the scapegoat, society's need to project its own bestial nature onto someone or something. The horns of the goat are representative of the Thanksgiving table centerpiece, the cornucopia symbolically emptying nature's bounty. The goat's horn can be also be used as a drinking vessel, which relates it to the wine festival.[3]

Government and Social Control

Saturn has to do with the rules and laws we live by. It represents civilizing power. Preserving the status quo is important to both Saturn and Capricorn. They are conservative, ordered, and traditional, interested in structure and stability. These attributes give Saturn and Capricorn their association with architecture and building design.

To function as a society, we need laws. Without an acceptance of the laws that tell us to stop at a red light and to go on a green light, there would be a lot more traffic accidents. Saturn is the law-and-order planet. It holds instinct in check. Problems come about with unequal enforcement of the traffic laws, and that is one of the problems with Saturn. Some communities adhere to a rigid enforcement of traffic laws, perhaps counting on that revenue to help balance the town budget. In other communities, enforcement is lax. Saturn can be weak or strong, rigid or flexible, a good cop or a bad cop.

Saturn is like the person who checks your coat and hat when you enter a club, keeping them until you're ready to leave. If we think of the hat and coat as our instincts, our raw ungoverned emotional tendencies, then we need Saturn to hold them in place so we don't lose control of them.

Saturn represents the law, but not everyone gets a thrill out of a traffic cop. William Golding's novel *Lord of the Flies* illustrates what can happen in a world without the restraint of Saturn. In this novel, a group of British schoolboys crash land on an island in the midst of a nuclear war. There are no adults. Left to their own devices and without the civilized structure of adult-imposed rules—Saturn—the boys slowly degenerate into savagery.

Saturn keeps us civilized enough so that the savagery on the freeway during the morning commute is kept to a minimum. Although everyone drives better when there is a traffic officer around, we still stop for the red lights even when there are no police.

Saturn is a conservative, restrictive planet. When restrictions and boundaries are imposed, some people react by rebelling, seeing it as freedom denied. When Pluto is added to the mix, as it will be in 2008, we will witness explosive rebellion against restrictions.

A Fear of Vastness, Losing Control, or Letting Go

Saturn is the boundary planet beyond which the outer planets orbit slowly through deep space. Saturn can sometimes be experienced as a fear of the unknown. In its most negative manifestation, it can be cold, rigid, and afraid of change.

On the other hand, it can also be a planet of solitude or renunciation. A strong Saturn can be experienced as positive loneliness, an embrace of the vast unknown. Poet William Wordsworth wrote of Saturnine loneliness enlightened by a moment of poetic and cosmic vision that connected earth and stars:

I wandered lonely as a cloud
That floats on high o'er vales and hills,
When all at once I saw a crowd,
A host, of golden daffodils;
Beside the lake, beneath the trees,
Fluttering and dancing in the breeze.
Continuous as the stars that shine
And twinkle on the milky way,
They stretched in never-ending line
Along the margin of a bay.[4]

Because of the fear of letting go, Saturn and Capricorn like to hold on to the past. The last time that Pluto was in Capricorn, in the 1760s and 1770s, Europe was enthralled by Greece's Golden Age; in the early American colonies, rapid changes and revolution led to intense nostalgia. The past is stable and reassuring. Starting in 2008, when Pluto enters Capricorn, an unprecedented wave of nostalgia will wash over us. This phenomenon may soon take several forms, including a renewed interest in preserving the past in museums and cultural venues.

Down-to-Earth, Hard-Headed Practicality

Saturn and Capricorn can both be hardworking and pragmatic. They are possessed of maturity and common sense, although their traditional competence can make them seem predictable.[5]

They are both associated with the business executive who can administer and get things done, thinking big and going after long-term goals. This side of Saturn and Capricorn demonstrates ambitious and determined organizational skill. It can sometimes manifest negatively as a callous ruthlessness in which the ends justify the means.

Both Saturn and Capricorn are good at figuring out solutions to tough jobs. They are down-to-earth and practical. Sun in Capricorn U.S. president Richard Nixon took practicality to an extreme and forgot about the means he was using to get re-elected. He focused on finding the right nuts and bolts, but lost sight of the democratic structure he was supposed to be representing. On the other hand, Nixon's practical, hard-headed approach to foreign affairs resulted in a policy that came to be called *realpolitik*. Dispensing with the ideological restraints of his Republican party, he shocked the world when he visited Communist China in 1972 and established a relationship that continues to grow and develop.

Writer and spiritual teacher Paramahansa Yogananda was another Capricorn who was strongly practical and knew how to get things done. In his autobiography, Yogananda relates how he built a worldwide organization in a foreign land out of nothing. The ability to organize, channel energies, and accomplish a large goal is one of the outstanding traits of Capricorn. They are great business and team managers. Yogananda was renowned for his practical and down-to-earth nature, and one of his avowed goals was to connect Eastern spirituality and Western practicality.[6]

Saturn and Capricorn are both patient. They can wait, and they are sometimes associated with aging and maturity, both of which will be important as the large Pluto in Leo population grows older. Issues surrounding old age will loom large in society as Pluto moves into Capricorn, starting in 2008.

Into the Future with Saturn and Capricorn

There are four traits associated with Saturn and Capricorn that will figure strongly in our futures. These traits will be introduced here, then discussed more fully in the next four chapters. In 2008, Pluto will go into the sign of Capricorn, activating transformation in the following areas:

- Security in all areas of life and culture will be strongly affected.
- A carnival atmosphere will surface as individuals and groups manifest the fins of the Capricorn goatfish.
- Masks will be used in ways literal and figurative—to hide, deceive, or shield.
- The self-made individual and supposed achiever of the American Dream will dominate the cultural landscape.

Security

Saturn and Capricorn are associated with security, already a looming concern in our lives because of terrorism.

Saturn operates a lot like anti-virus software on a computer. It is constantly scanning for problems. It monitors the environment, looking for threats. In fact, computer security will be one of the issues surging to the forefront when transforming Pluto moves into Capricorn in 2008.

Taking the anti-virus analogy a step further: imagine an unprotected computer, open to all manner of infections, viruses, and worms. That would be a world without the restraint of Saturn. Saturn helps us to monitor our surroundings. The mountain goat has to carefully scan the rocky crags before it leaps, just as we have to carefully scan our e-mails and downloads before opening them on our computers.

Saturn imposes order and discipline, and is a civilizing influence. It is the marshal with a badge, Wyatt Earp taming the Wild West.

When Saturn's influence is removed, chaos ensues. The boys in *Lord of the Flies* at first savored their Saturn-free existence on a jungle island. Then, without the civilizing influences of parents and teachers, they gradually descended into lawless tribes.

Bacchus

Another quality of Capricorn comes through the sign's association with Dionysus, the god of wine.[7] Dionysus, a Greek god, was the focus of a religious cult that worshipped and celebrated the fertility of nature. Dionysus is associated with revelry and release from prevailing moral strictures. In the Roman tradition, the equivalent of Dionysus was called Bacchus. A Roman celebration in honor of the god Saturn was called the Saturnalia or the Bacchanalia, a seven-day orgy of drinking and sensual pleasure.

The popularity of the original Greek Dionysian cult was a reaction to the increasing depiction of the gods as rational deities. Dionysus represented a rebellion against rational culture through sensory pleasures.[8] It is akin to a mountain goat (rational thought) with fins (sensory pleasures). Dionysus was worshipped by people who did not participate in the rational functions of society. The "haves" tend to enjoy Saturn's influence, since the laws usually protect what they have. It is the have-nots who grate against the structures that they feel disenfranchise them. Of course, this theme winds through all history. In our modern-day culture, there are many ways in which this Dionysian disenfranchisement will manifest, some of which will be discussed in chapter 6.

The Ascendant: Astrology Background

The Ascendant, the horizon at our moment of birth, also has to do with masks, but of a different sort. The Ascendant, how the world sees us, is figuratively more like a face than a mask. We can change masks, but our face is relatively permanent. A person with a Taurus Ascendant may not feel calm and placid, but that is how others often see someone with a Taurus Ascendant. If the Ascendant is our face to the world, it is one over which we do not have too much control, just as we don't have control over our Sun sign or Moon sign. That's who we are. Individuals can change and evolve, learn and grow, but the Sun, Moon, and Ascendant are our core identities.

Masks

Capricorn is associated with putting on a public mask. The sign has to do with how we choose to present ourselves to the world, the face we put on when we go to work or interact in any public way with others.

Capricorn is secure behind a social mask, scouring the immediate horizon for clues to ensure that the mask is effective. Although one does not need to be on stage to wear a mask, three prime examples of Sun in Capricorn performers with effective stage masks are Elvis Presley, *Seinfeld's* Julia Louis-Dreyfus, and Jim Carrey—who starred in *The Mask.*

Capricorn is also related to issues of integrity, of following a strict moral or ethical code of behavior. A person or institution with integrity must be vigilant to ensure that personal actions always proceed from central principles. A *dis*honest person also has to watch out, but for different reasons.

Integrity can be a good thing, but it can also result in superficial or hypocritical actions: a person tries to give a strong impression—a mask—of morality but is in fact immoral. George Orwell, in his novel *1984,* coined the word "doublethink" to describe a form of deception in which a lie is masked with such forceful terms of resolute honesty that it sounds true.[9] Imagine a little child expressing wide-eyed, emphatic denial for some misdemeanor for which he or she is actually guilty. Although Capricorn possesses a "polished social mask and a capacity to be at ease in the social world,"[10] a social mask can be used to conceal.

Saturn's orbit is the boundary between the inner and outer planets. Capricorn has to do with the difference between inner and outer forms[11] and the border between public and private. A Capricorn operating at a high level of integrity has dissolved the public-private boundary and is truly ethical; at this level, it's not an act but a genuine expression of the Capricorn's insides. Two shining Sun in Capricorn examples are Red Cross founder Clara Barton (see the Uranus-Neptune Profile at the end of chapter 10) and humanitarian Albert Schweitzer. If you scratch their surfaces, you'll find that their lives were expressions of their inner natures. When the highly evolved Capricorn's public mask is synchronized with his or her inner self, great things can happen because such individuals earn the enduring respect of the public.

Actress Diane Keaton became famous for playing Annie Hall, a role for which she won an Academy Award, in the Woody Allen movie of the same name. Keaton is a Capricorn Sun who wore a cinematic mask of charming, absent-minded insecurity. In interviews, it becomes apparent that in real life she is similar to, and yet different from, her screen persona. Keaton is an articulate, self-aware actress and artist, whose photos have been exhibited in museums and published in books. Other planets in her horoscope energize and influence her Capricorn Sun, giving it transparency. Audiences feel as if they are looking through pretty gauze at a captivating personality beneath the surface. Other factors in her horoscope help to give this appearance added depth and weight—audiences can sense a "there" in there. In 2003, Keaton received critical acclaim and an Oscar nomination for her role in *Something's Gotta Give,* in which she played an independent, successful playwright wooed by Jack Nicholson.

Diane Keaton: Astrology Background

Diane Keaton's charming, absent-minded quirkiness is explained by her conjunction of the Sun with Venus and Venus's exact square of Neptune. The Venus-Neptune square energizes her Capricorn Sun and makes her on-screen characters appear transparent, as though audiences can see right through her. Her Ascendant in Scorpio gives her depth, sex appeal, and an air of mystery.

The Self-Made Individual

Saturn and Capricorn also represent the more traditional, conservative qualities of the self-made individual, exemplified by Horatio Alger and the business executive. As Pluto moves into Capricorn, we will see a greater emphasis on entrepreneurial skill. Those who can strike off on their own and become successful by following their own "mountain paths" will be esteemed. The downside is that sometimes success is achieved by climbing over the backs of others. The world is filled with examples of individuals who succeeded on their own by being ruthless.

The American ideal has long been a Benjamin Franklin type of person, one who through hard work and skillful networking pulls himself or herself up by the bootstraps to become secure and successful. Franklin, an example of this practical and down-to-earth facet of Capricorn, will be discussed more fully in chapter 7. There is also a dark side to this American ideal, which can be seen in Don Vito Corleone, the fictional Mafia godfather. Corleone also worked hard and networked his way to the top, exhibiting many of those Saturnine qualities that are most prized in the American culture of self-achievement.

Capricorn Profile: Howard Hughes

Capricorn Howard Hughes, movie producer and business tycoon, wore a number of different masks. He was a pioneering aviation developer and the founder of Hughes Aircraft.

Saturn and Capricorn were dominant factors in his horoscope. It might seem unusual for someone so consumed with the air and air transport to have his Sun in an earth sign. Though he loved to fly, Howard Hughes was a true Capricorn, striving up the rocky industrial mountain. Flying was his freedom, but he always came back to earth.

Up until the age of eighteen, Hughes seemed to have no mind of his own. He appeared ready to submit to his father's educational expectations, and to follow his father in the family tool business. When first his mother and then his father died while he was in his late teens, Hughes inherited a fortune and exhibited for the first time the fierce independent ambition that was to characterize the rest of his life.

He had sure-footed self-confidence. When Hughes inherited his fortune, he quickly turned his back on his family home and business, and leapt out on his own to make movies in Hollywood.

Hughes was obsessive. In order to get ahead, it helps to have a sharp, one-pointed focus. Whatever Hughes did as a business executive, he did compulsively. This same character trait later crossed an invisible line into obsessive-compulsive disorder. When he was filming the aerial dogfight movie *Hell's Angels,* Hughes worked twenty-four and even thirty-six hours straight. He also exhibited the hard-headed business sense and deal-making aptitude for which Capricorn is renowned. As a film producer in the 1920s, he looked for every opportunity to get a better deal on a director's terms or a performer's salary.

A shy man, Hughes closely protected his privacy and revealed little of his inner self to the outer world. At parties, he could be observed with his head down, staring at his knuckles.[12]

Howard Hughes kept parts of himself secret from everyone. His drug addiction, which he kept a secret for most of his life, began with his recovery from a near-fatal plane accident.

Capricorn has a reclusive nature and is accustomed to donning masks when out in public. Hughes would slip into assumed identities to travel nomadically, spending time in various motels and hotels. Although mental illness and drug addiction are not characteristics of Capricorn—or any other zodiac sign, for that matter—Hughes had an undiagnosed mental illness, exacerbated or brought on by drug addiction. His obsessive need to be clean, which he seems to have got from his mother's over-concern with his physical well-being, dominated his later life.

Capricorn is cautious and wants to be secure from harm. One form of caution is to take measures to secure one's physical body. Hughes crossed over the line into paranoia and developed a fetish for sterile, germ-free environments.

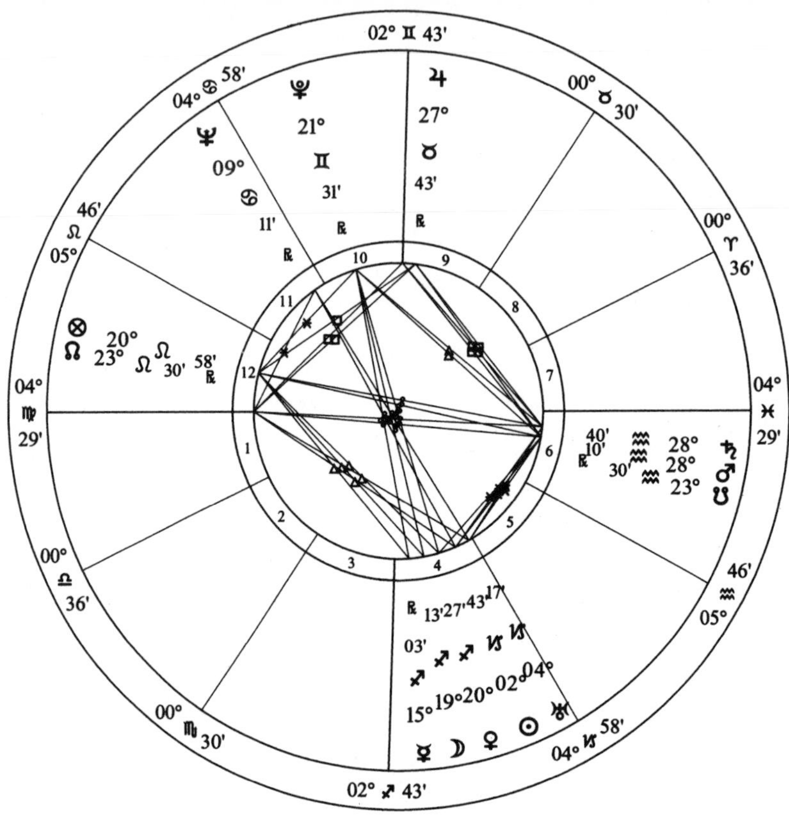

Howard Hughes
December 24, 1905 / 10:12 PM CST
Houston, Texas / Placidus houses

Howard Hughes: Astrology Background

Hughes's Sun was in Capricorn conjunct Uranus, giving him a fierce and striving individuality. He never followed the crowd. Mars and Saturn conjoined in Aquarius, a sign co-ruled in traditional astrology by Saturn. A whole book could be written on the markers for mental illness in Hughes's horoscope. His Neptune was opposite the Sun-Uranus conjunction—representing his escape from himself through film, airplanes, and obsessive-compulsive behavior. This seems to have been the dominant symbolism of his life. His Moon, representing his mother, opposed his natal Pluto.

Astro-Connection Activity

Capricorn Questions

Some questions to think about as we discuss Capricorn more fully in Part II of *Planet Trends*:

1. How will the Capricorn need for personal security manifest on a national and international level when Pluto enters the constellation of Capricorn in 2008?
2. Will security and safety become national or global obsessions?
3. To what extent will nations try to "sterilize" the environment?
4. How much will we project inner insecurities onto our world?

Endnotes

1. Deborah Houlding, "Capricorn: The Goatfish," Skyscript website, December 2003, http://www.skyscript.co.uk/cap_myth.html (accessed 22 August 2006).
2. Jean Chevalier and Alain Gheerbrant, *The Penguin Dictionary of Symbols,* trans. John Buchanan-Brown (New York: Penguin Books, 1996), 153.
3. The associations of the goat's horn in this paragraph are from Chevalier and Gheerbrant's *The Penguin Dictionary of Symbols,* pages 435 and 516.
4. William Wordsworth, "I Wandered Lonely as a Cloud," *The Norton Anthology of English Literature: Fifth Edition,* ed. M. H. Abrams (New York: W.W. Norton & Company), 206.
5. Skye Alexander, *Planets in Signs* (Atglen, Pennsylvania: Whitford Press, 1988), 62.
6. Paramahansa Yogananda, *Autobiography of a Yogi* (Los Angeles: Self-Realization Fellowship, 1968), 499.
7. Houlding, "Capricorn: The Goatfish."
8. Steven Kreis, "Nietzsche, Dionysus and Apollo," *The History Guide: Lectures on Twentieth Century Europe,* © 2000, Revised 13 May 2004, http://www.historyguide.org/europe/dio_apollo.html (accessed 22 August 2006).
9. George Orwell, *1984* (New York: New American Library, 1981), 176–177.
10. Wright, 29.
11. Wright, 28.
12. Donald L. Barlett and James B Steele, *Empire: The Life, Legend, and Madness of Howard Hughes* (New York: W. W. Norton & Company, 1979), 70.

CHAPTER 4

One If By Land: The New Age of Threat Levels

Conceal me what I am.

—Viola in Shakespeare's *Twelfth Night*

PLUTO	CAPRICORN
Powerful	Aging
Intense	Parental authority
Obsessive	Security and control
Exposing	Sensory pleasure
Transforming	Nostalgia
Extreme	Status Quo
Resourceful	Ambition
Probing	Protection
Secretive	Networking
	Social masks
	Big business
	Release of instinct

Citizens went about their daily lives in a state of high alert, and clandestine meetings took place under cover of darkness. Surveillance personnel were arrayed along the North Atlantic seaboard, scanning the dim horizon for signs of the enemy. A system of coded lights was set up to alert the defense forces.

Such was the scene in the days preceding the American Revolution when Paul Revere—a Sun in Capricorn—prepared to sound the alarm on his famous midnight ride.

The American Revolution was also the last time Pluto was in Capricorn. Astrological patterns repeat in cycles, and we will once again experience this transit starting in 2008 and lasting until 2024. Although we cannot count on historical events to reproduce themselves for the benefit of astrological cycles, larger themes from that earlier era will be repeated.

Horoscope for the United States: Astrology Background

Nations have horoscopes symbolizing their moment of birth, but astrologers disagree over the correct birth chart for the United States because of uncertainty over the time.[1] The house that a planet is in depends on the hour of day for which the chart is created. A widely used U.S. horoscope known as the Sibly chart places Pluto in the Second House. The Second House is the house of money, wealth, and status. Pluto in the Second House is appropriate for the wealthiest nation in the world. When Pluto returns to this "birth" point in the horoscope early in 2022, having taken almost two-and-a-half centuries to compete one cycle around the national horoscope, the nation may experience a powerful transformation of its wealth and status.The next four chapters are going to preview an era that has not yet arrived, demonstrating how Pluto's passage through Capricorn will affect trends large and small.

Pluto will be in Capricorn during the following time periods:

January 26, 2008–June 14, 2008
November 27, 2008–March 23, 2023
June 11, 2023–January 21, 2024
September 1, 2024–November 20, 2024

Starting in 2008, we will see a heightened stress on protection, control, and different levels of vigilance—national, personal identity, and digital. This chapter will forecast how cultural trends will be affected by the coming age of

Trend Versus Fad: Astrology Background

One way to ensure that a trend will last and is not just a passing fad is to match the trend with one or more of the major conjunctions in Parts III and IV of this book. The 2000 Jupiter-Saturn conjunction (see chapter 15) took place in the back-to-earth sign of Taurus—and Taurus is a sign associated with personal security.

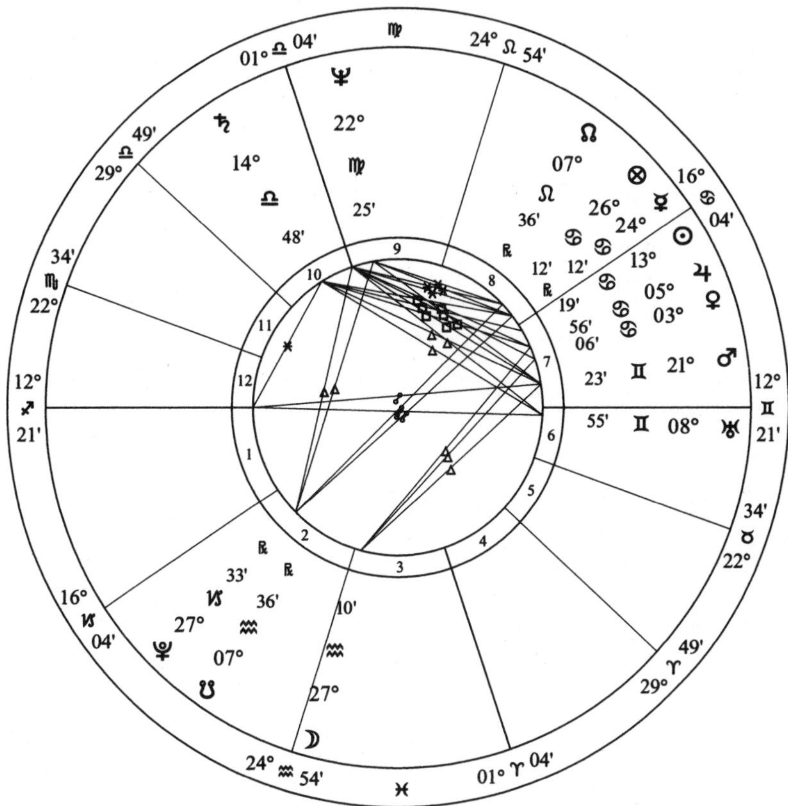

United States of America
July 4, 1776 / 5:10 PM LMT
Philadelphia, Pennsylvania / Placidus houses

high security. Pluto in Capricorn will bring a heavy emphasis on security and control; the tenor of the times will become more serious.

Here are major trends related to security starting in 2008, as predicted by Pluto's entry into Capricorn:

- A serious parental tone—and perhaps a strong "parent"—will urge the culture to replace its worn-out door locks.
- Government and corporate office buildings will become walled compounds.
- Architectural designs will reflect a heightened concern with security and preserving the past.
- Digital security barriers will be built—and breached.

- Biometric "chokepoints" will be set up at borders, worksites, and government buildings.
- Quarantines and masks to prevent the spread of contagious diseases will become more common.
- Hyper-vigilant and secure automobiles will hit the road.
- Moral walls will be erected to keep out an explosion of carnival revelry and debauchery.
- Data mining—the extraction of useful information hidden in large databases—will become a powerful personal security issue.

Ushering in a More Serious Tone

Underlying the trend toward tighter security will be a more serious tone. Capricorn is the sign most often associated with parental authority, and when Pluto enters Capricorn, it will be like a parent coming home early and interrupting the teenage Sagittarius party. A serious parental tone may manifest in the following ways:

- A cautious collective parent installs extra deadbolts to keep the family safe at night.
- A suspicious parent scrutinizes every friend that his children bring home and then bars the doors on the outside so the children can't leave.
- Parents in the Pluto in Leo generation—those born between 1939 and 1958, forever children at heart no matter how old they become—will seek to reconnect with children they have lost to divorce and separation.
- A national or international series of events more severe than the events of September 11, 2001, will create a serious tone and heightened security.

Pluto in Capricorn symbolizes a strong parent. For example, Chinese Communist dictator Mao Zedong—a Capricorn Sun—was the father of his country; he exercised a strong parental hand in China's modern development. During Pluto's transit through Capricorn, a nation may install a strong parental leader, one who is able to keep order and discipline.

Skyscraper Security

Thick, blast-proof walls and barriers will soon be permanent features of the commercial landscape. Government and corporate office buildings will become walled compounds.

Multinational corporations have become terrorist targets, making concrete barriers a common sight around businesses and government buildings at home and abroad. These concrete barriers will be replaced by more aesthetic—yet still blast-proof—security walls. As Pluto enters Capricorn, the sign of the architect, the integration of blast-resistant security elements into actual building design will become commonplace.

Mythologist Joseph Campbell said that a culture's dominant values are reflected in its tallest buildings.[2] Our skyscrapers extol commerce, but after 2008 they will also exalt protection. Freedom Tower, envisioned as the first in a series of towers on the site of the World Trade Center, will overlook a planned 9/11 memorial. Freedom Tower is due to be completed in 2009 or 2010, just as Pluto settles into Capricorn. Freedom Tower's height—1776 feet—will be a symbolic link to the nation's birth. Pluto's passage through Capricorn, where that distant planet was traveling in 1776, will similarly create an astrological bond to the United States' collective past.

The Astrology of Architecture

Capricorn likes the past. Cultural venues, art museums, and libraries are dedicated to preserving and exhibiting the past. The modern museum has become a commercial as well as a cultural center in cities. During Pluto's passage through Capricorn, we will see this trend accelerate. Museums will proliferate and, in keeping with the symbolism of Capricorn, they won't just preserve the past as the Guggenheim Museum in Bilbao, Spain, and concert venues such as Disney Hall in Los Angeles—both designed by Frank Gehry, whose liquid designs reflect his Pisces Sun—will continue to be the most original in the architectural world.

Freedom Tower will be a shimmering, glass-encased skyscraper topped by a spire designed to suggest the Statue of Liberty. Security will be a paramount concern. Included in Freedom Tower will be a concrete core, steel-cable netting that will brace the building, chemical and biological filters, extra-strong fireproofing, areas of refuge on each floor, and blast-resistant glazing in the lobby.[3] We can expect to see similar security elements used in a wide variety of public buildings.

When completed, Freedom Tower will be the world's tallest building. If Joseph Campbell's words hold true, our highest values will start to be reflected in the commemoration of the fallen, which will reflect Pluto's passage into the most serious of the twelve astrological signs.

Digital Barriers, Big Brother, and Digital Spying

Capricorn is ruled by Saturn, the planet considered to be the boundary between the inner and the outer planets. This lends Capricorn an association with boundaries and borders, the security of which is a growing concern in the post-9/11 world.

In the modern information age, however, security barriers are often invisible. Computer users, for example, often employ a firewall to protect their computers from outside intruders. Computer and Internet security will continue to grow in importance, reaching a crucial tipping point during the early part of Pluto's transit through Capricorn.

In Greek mythology, Argus was a hundred-eyed surveillance monster created by Zeus's wife, Hera, to guard Io, with whom Zeus had an adulterous affair. A Plutonian mixture of sex and secret monitoring is already beginning to surface in the culture. It will become much more widespread when Pluto enters Capricorn. A suspicious spouse can now install secret Argus-like software that will monitor a loved one's every keystroke on the computer and capture each Internet image.

Argus is similar to the Big Brother security in *1984*, George Orwell's anti-totalitarian novel. In this novel, "telescreens" are interactive eyes through which private activity is monitored by the government. The telescreen is akin to our modern interactive screen, the home computer. Businesses have become the primary eyes into the private lives of consumers. Many online businesses place small tracking bots on personal computers to follow and record computer users' every move. Capricorn is the sign of big business, and when Pluto enters this sign, the business monitoring of privacy through different types of surveillance will surface as a powerful issue.

Capricorn is associated with security, caution, and hypervigilance. It is cautious and monitors the environment. Britain has so many security cameras that a person's every public move can now be tracked, an omnipresent vigilance that enabled British authorities to identify the July 7, 2005, London Underground terrorist bombers on closed-circuit television.

When Pluto enters Capricorn in 2008, this type of surveillance will escalate. Pluto in Capricorn will bring much more surveillance of individuals through the use of the Global Positioning System (GPS), which is finding new applications all the time. Global positioning technology will be used to track people—even when they don't know it. The GPS embedded in mobile phones allows employers to use the satellite network to make sure workers are where they say they are. Parents will also make use of GPS technology to check up on teenage children. And husbands and wives can clandestinely track errant spouses using GPS.

The Softer Side of Security

As the world becomes a more dangerous place and security becomes tighter, people will look for ways to soften their lives. One way to soften is through color. In 2004, the color pink suddenly blossomed as a fashion rage, due in part to the hard-edged times in which we live. People are looking for ways to soften their lives and breathe some Sagittarian optimism into clothing accessories. Pink breast cancer awareness ribbons have also received more prominent display, indicating a surge of feminine consciousness in culture, as well as a move away from the egalitarian fashion statements of Neptune in Aquarius (see chapter 11). Pink is the stereotypical "girl's color," now being subverted as a statement of Plutonian power.

We will see other subversive softening trends in the retail market as Pluto moves closer to, and into, Capricorn. These might include items such as fluffy scarves or comfort foods. Knitting could make a comeback.

Biometric Security

Biometrics is the use of unique physical markers for personal identification. A new type of biometric wall uses technology to read biological traits—a person's fingerprints, hand, or face. Secure worksites, borders, and government buildings will soon allow access only through doorways—known in true Capricorn nomenclature as "chokepoints"—that employ biometric security devices. When Pluto enters Capricorn, a sign associated with boundaries and security, biometrics will become widespread. Stores, fast-food outlets, and even some gambling casinos are already starting to employ biometrics for payment identification. Biometrics will soon replace plastic debit cards and credit cards. Customers will be able to swipe a finger instead of a card.

This is also intended as a step in the fight against identity theft. One can hope that it would be much easier to steal a credit card or Social Security number than a finger or an eyeball. In the futurist movie *Minority Report,* optical scanners identify each person's unique eyeballs. The main character, played by Tom Cruise, undergoes an operation to replace his eyeballs as a painful means of identity theft. Biometric identification will have interesting repercussions in the evolving world of identity theft.

Quarantines and Masks

Quarantines to prevent the global spread of diseases will be another type of secure barrier erected during Pluto's passage through Capricorn. Our connected world means that diseases that were once easy to contain now spread rapidly. The outbreak of severe acute respiratory syndrome (SARS) in 2003—and its containment through draconian quarantines—was a harbinger of future globe-trotting diseases. Pluto in Sagittarius coupled with Neptune in Aquarius has led to the rapid spread of global disease. Pluto in Capricorn will bring disease-resistant walls, including quarantines and mass vaccines. Masks are an important part of Pluto in Capricorn and will be discussed in chapter 7. However, it is worth mentioning here that we will see much more frequent wearing of surgical masks as disease barriers.

Barriers will be incorporated in new materials. Nanotechnology is the science of manipulating matter at the molecular level, and is already being used in some manufacturing processes. It will become much more common as Pluto moves into Capricorn. Stain-resistant trousers use nanotechnology, creating barriers in the clothing material. Anti-glare windows also use nanotechnology.

Mountain-Goat Cars

Automobiles during Pluto's years in Capricorn will become safe, agile, hypervigilant vehicles. Think of the car of the future—already on the drawing boards because it can take years to go from automobile concept to factory production—as a mountain goat. Tires will be like nimble, sure-footed hooves, able to sense and adjust for the slightest changes in road conditions. Smart highways will monitor traffic flow and road conditions, communicating this information to a vehicle's navigation system.

Some cars and trucks will sport such an array of safety and security devices that they will be like traveling fortresses. The Pluto in Capricorn vehicle will have enhanced vision. Infrared technology will allow a car to scan the darkness, and cars will soon have radar-equipped cruise control to detect following distance and adjust the speed. Side radar on cars will "see" in the driver's blind spot. Future cars will be equipped with a sensor that wakes sleepy drivers by monitoring body temperature, and digital cameras built into cars will monitor traffic. The Global Positioning System will become more interactive, and drivers will be able to use GPS to navigate around traffic congestion and accidents. By 2010, cars will have systems that will be able to detect an accident just before it happens and allow the driver to take appropriate evasive action.[4]

Chapter 7 will discuss the Benjamin Franklin-like qualities of Pluto in Capricorn, one of which is a proliferation of practical inventions to assist people in ordinary tasks. The Pluto in Capricorn automobile will use a number of these practical, applied technologies.

Moral Walls

Looking ahead to Pluto's transit through Capricorn, the more traditional qualities of the sign seem to point in the direction of increased restraint and civility. While we will indeed see more restriction, some of the barriers will be legal and moral guards against a marauding dissolute faction in popular culture.

Saturn and Capricorn are not just associated with Ben Franklin. Radio personality Howard Stern, a Sun in Capricorn, reveals another side of this sign—the release of the primal adolescent. The hormonal side of Capricorn, which will be discussed in detail in the next chapter, will provoke strong reactions from institutional parents and guardians. Barriers against a perceived cultural immorality will go up in Congress and in the media. Walls, both literal and figurative, will be raised.

Data Mining

Pluto rules mining, probing deep below the surface. Saturn, Capricorn's ruler, also rules mining through its association with heavy earth.

A digital form of mining known as data mining—the extraction of information hidden in large databases—will become a major security issue as Pluto enters Capricorn.

The most common form of data mining is done by supermarkets when they use an individual shopper discount card to track purchasing patterns. When shopping at the local supermarket, a customer is presented with a computer-generated coupon for a *future* purchase based on what he or she just bought. Bar coding of products has also enabled purchases to be grouped with others in a large database to help the supermarket determine purchasing patterns. A supermarket may want to know which items are bought in combination, say, or at the express checkout counter.

Capricorn is the sign of big business organizations. Pluto's entry into this sign signifies a new corporate era—and its problems. Large retailers now rely on computer systems to track inventory and customer behavior. This data can be mined for retailing gold. Data mining, like Pluto, reveals what's hidden. Wal-Mart has an unrivaled customer database. When Wal-Mart executives wanted to know what to stock up on in Florida Wal-Marts before a hurricane struck in 2004, they came up with forecasts based on what had sold during the previous hurricane. Sure, flashlights and candles were big sellers. But, they discovered, so were Pop-Tarts and beer. So the Wal-Mart stores in the hurricane path received extra deliveries of Pop-Tarts and six-packs.[5]

This common and benign mining of customer data is at the forefront of a national debate over privacy. It will become a big issue when Pluto enters Capricorn because databases will have expanded, along with software's ability to mine that data. We could see a time when the accumulated bits and bytes of our lives—from supermarket purchases to airplane tickets to Amazon.com transactions—are placed into a giant database, allowing a future individual, corporation, or government entity to have near-total insight into our private lives.

Endnotes

1. The early U.S. leaders did not keep detailed records as Congress does today, and so the time of the official ratification of the Declaration of Independence is today a matter of conjecture. Not all astrologers use the Sagittarius-rising Sibly chart (named for an astrologer who drew up the first known horoscope of the U.S.) Some favor a Virgo-rising chart, others Gemini-rising, and still others Scorpio-rising. No matter which horoscope one uses, however, if it's for July 4, 1776, the Sun and all the planets will be in the same degree. Only the Moon will vary within a few degrees.
2. Joseph Campbell, *The Power of Myth with Bill Moyers* (New York: Doubleday, 1988), 94–97.
3. Lower Manhattan Construction Command Center website, http://www.lowermanhattan.info/construction/project_updates/freedom_tower_26204.aspx (accessed 22 August 2006).
4. John Roach, "Locusts Inspire Technology That May Prevent Car Crashes," *National Geographic News*, 6 August 2004, http://news.nationalgeographic.com/news/2004/08/0806_040806_locusts.html (accessed 22 August 2006).
5. Constance L. Hays, "What They Know About You," *The New York Times*, 14 November 2004, http://www.nytimes.com/2004/11/14/business/yourmoney/14wal.html (accessed 22 August 2006).

CHAPTER 5

Blowing a Carnival Horn

What was he doing, the great god Pan,
Down in the reeds by the river?
Spreading ruin and scattering ban,
Splashing and paddling with hoofs of a goat . . .
—Elizabeth Barrett Browning, "A Musical Instrument"

. . . an admirable evasion
of whoremaster man, to lay his goatish
disposition to the charge of a star.
—William Shakespeare, *King Lear*

At the height of the Roman Empire, a scribe named Petronius wrote the *Satyricon,* which satirized the excesses of Nero's Rome while portraying a sexually liberated culture. The satyr is a mythic creature, half goat and half man. It is associated with Greek wine festivals, randy behavior, and the zodiac sign of Capricorn. In the *Satyricon,* gender identities were fluid and the satyr of the title symbolized an overindulgent Roman culture. At the time, around AD 50, Pluto was in Capricorn.

Although Pluto in Capricorn can symbolize the release of instincts, it can also signify the opposite—the cultural or political repression of licentious behavior. During Pluto's last passage through Capricorn, between 1762 and 1778, American Puritanism kept a heavy lid on cultural excess.

At the same time that American Puritanism was in full force, something entirely different was happening in France. There, the overindulgent excesses of royal, upper-class French culture had become so extreme that a class revolution was beginning to boil.

A Capricorn Rogues' Gallery

Yes, it's true, Benjamin Franklin was a Capricorn. But so are radio personality Howard Stern, disgraced televangelist Jim Bakker, and car designer John DeLorean. Capricorn has its secrets, too. Here is a rogues gallery of three Capricorns who managed their own party-animal scenes—or behind-the-scenes parties.

#1—Shock jock **Howard Stern** is a radio host who specializes in crossing the lines of propriety. He represents a release of the unbridled libido that can occur with Capricorn. Howard Stern personifies the ribald energies of the sophomoric male id (the id is a Freudian term representing the unconscious center of wants and needs, pleasures and desires—our deepest sexual and aggressive motives.) His battle with the Federal Communications Commission is representative of a more general cultural battle to control licentious behavior. This conflict will intensify as Pluto moves into Capricorn. Major cultural trends do not come out of nowhere. They build momentum and—depending on the trend—come to a head during an outer planet's passage through a particular sign.

#2—Jim Bakker. He was the Capricorn TV minister who had it all: good looks; charm;

When Pluto is in Capricorn, instincts can become liberated, repressed, or violent.

This chapter will spotlight the earthy side of Capricorn, forecasting trends associated with a side of Capricorn that, in the words of astrologer Paul Wright, releases "the lusty, exuberant, and sometimes violent side of human nature."[1]

A Capricorn Rogues' Gallery: Astrology Background

Howard Stern: Howard Stern's horoscope has three planets—the Sun, Mercury, and Venus—in Capricorn. These three planets form part of a highly energized Grand Cross. A Grand Cross is two sets of opposition planets whose axes square one another. Howard Stern's Capricorn planets are closely opposed by Uranus in the Third House of communication, allowing him to project an eccentric, rebellious, and uninhibited on-air persona. This opposition is squared by the axis of another opposition, between Neptune and a Taurus Moon, showing the boyish craving for sensual gratification. Mars in sex-obsessed Scorpio completes the picture of the eternal adolescent.

Jim Bakker: The most significant aspect in Jim Bakker's horoscope is a very close square of his Capricorn Sun with Saturn. This makes the issue of control—of himself and others—a central issue in his life. The issues of a Capricorn Sun are strengthened and exacerbated by the square to Saturn. In addition, Mercury squares Neptune, symbolizing deceptive communications, while his exalted Taurus Moon opposes a Scorpio Venus.

John DeLorean: His Capricorn Sun is part of a T-square with Mars and Pluto, with Mars as the middle planet. This gave him a great deal of aggressive energy and an excessive need to control.

It is important to note, however, that this roguish display of Capricorn is far outweighed by those Capricorns who exhibit sober, mature, responsible citizenship. The list of famous Capricorns who do good in the world, some of whom are noted elsewhere in this book, is long and considerable.

Capricorn Forecasts

When Pluto enters Capricorn in 2008, we can expect to see trends in the following areas:

- The normal social hierarchies will be upended.
- Marriage and gender roles and rules will be transformed.
- There will be a relaxing of the normal inhibitions and rules of behavior. Certain uninhibited parts of culture will be figuratively walled off, accompanied by a strong moral backlash.

millions of dollars in spending money, in the early 1980s, from devoted TV parishioners; the Heritage USA amusement park; luxury cars; mansions; numerous bank accounts; a private jet; and marriage to Tammy Faye Bakker. He claimed they were all gifts from God.[2] But Jim Bakker's televangelist ministry came apart when it was revealed that he had tried to pay the church secretary, Jessica Hahn, $265,000 in hush money to keep their adulterous affair a secret. He was eventually tried and convicted on twenty-three counts of fraud and one count of conspiracy for stealing donations from his PTL ministry.

#3—John DeLorean, who died in 2005, was an automobile executive and entrepreneur who designed the self-named DeLorean, a uniquely styled stainless steel sports car with gull wing doors. The DeLorean car became even more famous when it was used in the movie *Back to the Future*. DeLorean tried to raise money for his fledgling automobile company by smuggling cocaine. Although an infamous grainy video caught him making a drug deal, DeLorean was later acquitted when he charged the authorities with entrapment.

Outrageous Satur(n)day Night Men's Fashion Forecasts for 2010:

- High heels
- Three-quarters-length tight jeans
- Modified jester hats
- Bubblegum pink, sunshine yellow, and lime green blazers

An Upside-Down World

Starting in about 2008, older generations will cavort like teenagers and teenagers will behave like sober, circumspect adults. Internet dating will become the domain of senior citizens.

Capricorn is associated with the Bacchinalian revel (see chapter 3). We will see good old-fashioned booze reassert its dominance as a freer of inhibitions, which doesn't seem to fit the usual view of Capricorn. We tend to see Capricorn as a sign of top-down management, propriety, and sobriety. Capricorn is all of these, but it is an earth sign ruled by Saturn, which gave us Satur(n)day, the one day of the week in Western culture given over to self-indulgence and freedom from weekday restraint.[3]

Capricorn is closely related to the figure of Pan (see page 37), a satyr associated with fertility worship. In the movie *William Shakespeare's Romeo and Juliet,* Juliet's father dresses as a lecherous Pan-like character for a costumed debauch. This scene could serve as a metaphor for the eruption of the id that will take place once Pluto moves into Capricorn. This is not to suggest that all Capricorns are horny goats. Very often, they are most in control of that part of the psyche—because they know and understand its power.

Twelfth Night

One of the twentieth century's most influential philosophers, Mikhail Bakhtin, believed that the carnival embodied many of a culture's richest elements. During the traditional carnival, people are allowed to violate decorum, ridicule officialdom without fear of reprisal, and celebrate physical excess.

In William Shakespeare's comedy *Twelfth Night,* the world is turned on its ear. The play, subtitled *What You Will,* is set on the twelfth day after Christmas. The Elizabethan Twelfth Night, celebrated while the Sun was in Capricorn, was a carnival-like holiday during which excessive and licentious behavior were condoned. Old rules were suspended and people were freed from traditional social roles. The servant was given liberty to usurp the master or mistress, and a normally staid world of very clear class distinctions became, if only for a day, an upside-down world of lusty and mischievous misbehavior.

Twelfth Night illustrates so much of this carnival side of Capricorn that it is worth recounting its basic plot and themes, many of which will surface in our culture when Pluto enters Capricorn. Some future cultural trends to watch for, embodied in the play, are masks, gender confusion, disguises, and the suspension of old rules.

In *Twelfth Night,* two young-adult identical twins are accidentally separated in a strange land. One twin is a young woman, Viola; the other is her brother, Sebastian. Viola disguises herself as a man in order to survive unaccompanied in the strange land. She finds employment with the local duke, with whom she quickly falls in love but is unable to profess that love because of her disguise. The duke, it turns out, is in love with a noblewoman named Olivia. The duke asks Viola to bring a love message to Olivia. However, Olivia, upon meeting Viola and mistaking her for a young man, falls in love with her.

In Shakespeare's day, female roles were played by boys. Sexist though this convention may have been, it allowed Shakespeare to have fun with his theme of mistaken identity. The character of Viola would have been played by a boy who acted the part of a young woman who then donned the disguise of a young man, causing another woman to fall in love with him/her/him. And he/she/he is in love with the duke, who in turn loves Olivia. Meanwhile, Olivia accidentally runs into Viola's twin brother Sebastian, and mistaking him for Viola, promptly marries Sebastian (who really *is* a man).

A secondary plot involves the servants, a drunken uncle in Olivia's house, and Olivia's overbearing steward. The servants and the inebriated uncle comically attempt to get even with Malvolio, the pompous, self-righteous manager of wealthy Olivia's household. The servants turn the tables on Malvolio when they get him to make a public fool out of himself and then imprison him for being insane.

In the end, sobriety returns and the proper hierarchy is restored, albeit with changed perspectives by all.

A carnival atmosphere will come alive as Pluto moves into Capricorn. Satirizing and making fun of the powerful will thrive as forms of delicious humor, but these jokes will not be appreciated by the objects of derision. When Pluto enters Capricorn, the Malvolios of the world will become more and more transparent and open to ridicule. They will also behave like *Twelfth Night's* Malvolio, becoming entrenched in their own behavior and ego. Someone who is in charge and is the butt of ridicule tends to strike back, so Pluto in Capricorn can become repressive.

Think of *Twelfth Night* as the Elizabethan Renaissance version of today's anonymous Internet chat rooms, in which gender confusion reigns. The sex-role subversion of *Twelfth Night* is played out today in some sex chat rooms where individuals try to mask their genders, pretending to be the opposite sex to lure unsuspecting chat room visitors into same-sex encounters—or vice versa. When Pluto goes into Capricorn, this confusing gender masking and sexual-identity switching will become more mainstream.

We can expect more expression of Dionysus, the god of the wine festival and a character associated with Capricorn. Bacchanalian rites, satyrs, and nymphs will become lively elements in the culture. The 2004 movie *Sideways*, about a wine-soaked week during which two friends either repress or release their inhibitions, previewed some of the contrasting possibilities of Pluto in Capricorn.

We will see the release of the Freudian id in parts of the culture. Normal inhibitions and rules of behavior will be relaxed, and some will express the earthier side of Pluto's transit through Capricorn.

Astrologer Paul Wright notes that one facet of Capricorn is an "expression of an overcivilized culture seeking the revitalizing sustenance of pagan roots."[4] He relates Capricorn—an earth sign—to the primal expression of rock music. Wright mentions the example of Annie Lennox—the short-haired singer who recorded albums titled *Savage*, *Medusa*, and *Bare*, as well as a song called "Primitive." Lennox is also famous for bending genders in her stage persona and for delivering songs with a voice that seems to have enough power to carry notes to the moon and stars.

Another Capricorn who expressed this release through rock music was Elvis Presley. His leg and pelvic shaking was even reminiscent of a spindly-legged mountain goat balanced on hind quarters, preparing to leap.

Certain enclaves will permit outrageous behavior. Las Vegas is positioning itself as party central in time for Pluto in Capricorn. In fact, a visit to Las Vegas today can be a walk on the wild side. The Internet is also doing its part to foster this culture. Beginning in 2008, there will be new pre-gentrified Times Squares, sections of modern culture that will be walled off and set aside for blowing carnival horns, accompanied by a public backlash against the perceived growth in immorality.

A somewhat related development will be the increased interest in pagan religions and rituals. Individuals and groups will seek to revitalize themselves by adopting pre-Christian worship practices.

Endnotes

1. Paul Wright. *Astrology in Action.* (Sebastopol, California: CRCS Publications, 1989), 28.
2. Jim Bakker's extravagant lifestyle is detailed in Charles E. Shepard's book *Forgiven: The Rise and Fall of Jim Bakker and the PTL Ministry* (New York: Atlantic Monthly Press, 1989).
3. Wright, 28.
4. Wright, 109.

Chapter 6

"Who's There?" Seeing Behind the Mask

We penetrated deeper and deeper into the heart of darkness.
—Joseph Conrad, *Heart of Darkness*

Who's there?
—William Shakespeare, the opening line of *Hamlet*

Capricorn has to do with wearing a social mask. Many people wear masks to conceal certain facets of themselves that they aren't comfortable sharing with others, but with Capricorn it is different. Capricorn wears a mask as a means to an end. For example, a salesperson making a sales call may have just had a fight with a spouse or a partner. Yet during the sales pitch, the salesperson is cheerful, optimistic, and smiling. It's not that the salesperson is trying to conceal emotions; she just wants to make a sale and, to do that, she must connect with others in a positive manner. It's part of the job.

Capricorn represents a smooth, goal-focused, self-abnegating willingness to dissemble. It need not be ruthless or manipulative, although it can be. Our hypothetical salesperson may be selling swampland or a useful product we really need. Either way, the sale does not get made if the salesperson is negative and pessimistic.

Spiderman and Peter Parker

The 2004 movie *Spiderman 2* illustrates some of the issues we will be dealing with when Pluto goes into Capricorn. The movie's plot hinges on Peter Parker's need to shed his mask and merge his two separate identities. Spiderman is Peter Parker's crime-fighting alter ego. As Peter Parker, he is a gawky, bumbling teenager. His personal life is brimming with insecurity and teen angst. Wearing the mask of Spiderman, however, he saves lives, rescues children, and catches criminals. Capricorn, remember, is the sign of the mask we wear when we are fulfilling our public role.

As it turns out, his superhero mask creates the need for another Peter Parker mask to hide that one. This will be the story of Pluto in Capricorn—masks within masks, like little wooden Russian dolls. Finding a person's true identity will become difficult, if not impossible. Peter Parker becomes overwhelmed with the effort necessary to carry on a double life. He tries hard to hold back the rising waters of his psyche, but they eventually crest and spill over into his superhero life. When Pluto enters Capricorn, we too will have a more difficult time hiding our private lives behind masks, individually and collectively.

When Pluto enters Capricorn, there will be a great urge to shed masks, to be authentic. In some cases, masks will be removed involuntarily. As will be noted in J. Edgar Hoover's Astrology Background (see page 72), his law-enforcement mask may not have been able to survive Pluto in Capricorn. During this upcoming transit, powerful individuals will be unmasked.

Although scandal has always been a part of fame and power, what will be important when Pluto goes into Capricorn is how the powerful react to seeing masks pulled from their own public faces.

There are several ways Pluto in Capricorn will bring masks to the cultural surface:

- Powerful hypocrites, accustomed to being able to control and conceal, will be exposed.
- The merging of private sexual orientations with the courageous public statement of same-sex marriage will provoke strong reactions.
- Individuals will cultivate multiple identities, names, and masks.
- There will be a great urge to shed masks, to be authentic.
- Electronic masks will be used to disguise and conceal.
- Identity theft and related crimes will surge.
- The collective psyche will shudder under the weight of too much compartmentalizing.
- Intense, heart-rending nostalgia will mask difficult and uncertain times in the world.

- The masking of power and the use of clever strategies to conceal a winning hand will manifest in international relations and world conflict.

Hypocrisy, the Dark Side of Capricorn

Capricorn involves establishing a sense of integrity so that our public and private selves are in harmony. Private behavior can cause serious problems if it conflicts with the face we exhibit in public. Capricorn is about making the two selves one, or at least being able to walk like one talks. Pluto in Capricorn will therefore not be pleasant for hypocrites who happen to be caught in the sudden glare of the limelight. The prime example of this is the conservative politician who criticizes anyone who fails to support family values, rails against the lack of morality in others, and then gets caught having an adulterous affair. In some cases, the exposure of a secret private life can be ruinous for a public career.

Judge Pyncheon, a character in Nathaniel Hawthorne's *The House of the Seven Gables,* wears an impressive social mask. He exhibits purity, faithfulness, and devotedness, as well as a "rigid consistency." He was renowned for "the severity with which he had frowned upon, and finally cast off, an expensive and dissipated son, delaying forgiveness until within the final quarter of an hour of the young man's life." Judge Pyncheon supported the temperance movement while confining himself to "just" five glasses of sherry each day. His cane was gold-headed, his boots polished, and his smile benevolent.[1] In short, he was a certified American hypocrite, filled with false rectitude. He is part of a masked line that descends down through Suns in Capricorn Jim Bakker and J. Edgar Hoover. When Pluto enters Capricorn, the covers will be pulled from some worshipped public figures.

J. Edgar Hoover, who had a very strong Capricorn in his horoscope, was appointed director of the Federal Bureau of Investigation in 1924 and served in that position until he died in 1972—spending almost five decades as the nation's chief law enforcer. During that time, he transformed the FBI into the nation's premier law enforcement agency. The FBI's G-men became synonymous with white hats and rooting out crime. At the same time, Hoover used the FBI to collect private information on politicians and others in power—information that he then used to manipulate or persecute. He was an intensely private, even secretive, man. Speculation and rumors that Hoover was gay and a secret cross-dresser have never been confirmed.

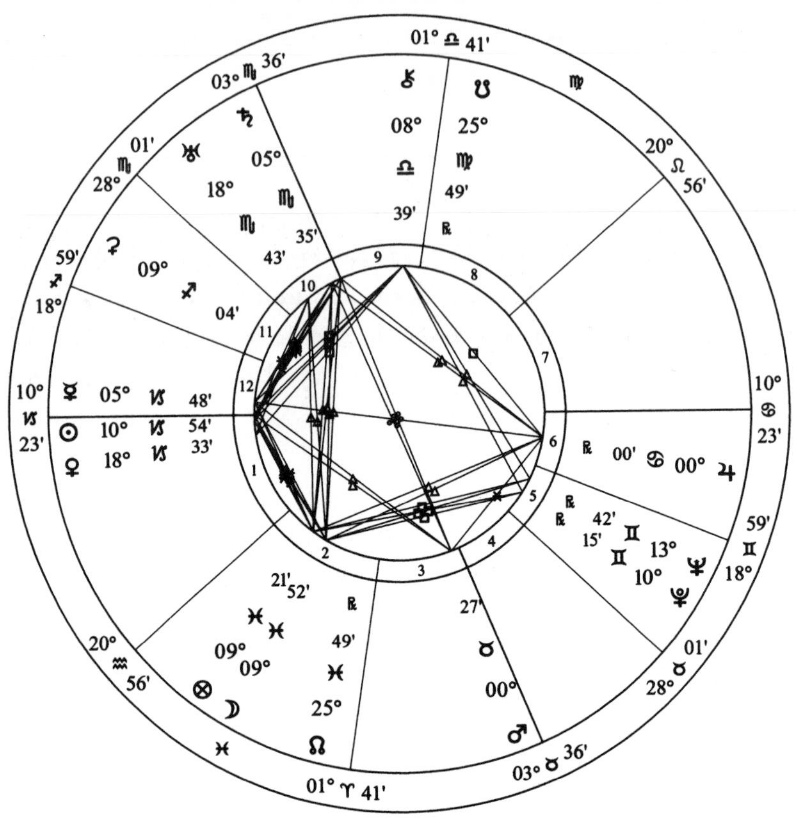

J. Edgar Hoover
January 1, 1895 / 7:30 AM EST
Washington, D.C. / Placidus houses

J. Edgar Hoover: Astrology Background

Three Capricorn planets—the Sun, Mercury, and Venus—clustered around Hoover's Ascendant, giving him extraordinary Capricorn power and a strong, impenetrable Capricorn mask. The Ascendant is the way we are perceived by others. One manifestation of a Capricorn Ascendant is an enforcement-type personality, trying to keep things in check all the time. Hoover had Saturn in Scorpio conjunct the Midheaven, which further symbolized his law-enforcement tendencies. This, along with his Capricorn planets on the Ascendant, made him the *law*. His intercepted Pisces Moon, somewhat bereft in the Second House of self-worth, seems overpowered by the square from Pluto on one side and Ceres on the other. Intense and unresolved childhood issues drove him in life. The focal House, where Hoover's Moon sought release from the stress, was the emotional, private, and watery Eighth House. He might not have been able to take his secrets to the grave if Pluto had been in Capricorn, where it would cross over his Ascendant and Sun.

Steve Garvey: Astrology Background

In addition to the Sun, Steve Garvey has three other planets in Capricorn—including aggressive Mars and sporty Jupiter.

Former professional baseball player Steve Garvey, another Capricorn Sun, also wore a public mask. He and his wife Cyndy became known as "Ken and Barbie" for their wholesome good looks and resemblance to the Mattel doll duo. Steve Garvey seemed to embody many stalwart Capricorn traits. He was hardworking, tenacious, ambitious, strong, consistent, and persistent. As the first baseman for the Los Angeles Dodgers, Garvey won the National League's Most Valuable Player Award in 1974. He also holds the National League record for most consecutive games played. In addition to his baseball statistics, Steve Garvey projected a wholesome, Mr. Clean sports image that at times seemed like a throwback to a bygone era of larger-than-life sports heroes. He was nicknamed "The Senator" by teammates.

However, in the 1980s two paternity suits and a tell-all book by his ex-wife Cyndy revealed that there was a lot the public had not seen. Garvey's wholesome mask hid a host of personal character defects. Once considered a potential candidate for statewide or even national office, Garvey instead became the tarnished host of game shows and infomercials.[2] Capricorn has a facility for public display that is not always matched by inner character.

Same-Sex Marriage

The transit of Pluto in Sagittarius has brought same-sex marriage to the surface, and this issue will resonate even more loudly when Pluto enters Capricorn because it involves the public versus the private self and the merging of one's nature with a public identity.[3] Marriage is a public bond and commitment. Our sexual orientation, however, is a private matter. So when a same-sex couple marries, their public and private selves are joined in a way that is different from a heterosexual marriage. For a same-sex couple to marry, then, is still an act of quiet courage.

When Pluto crosses into Capricorn—just after the 2008 U.S. presidential election—same-sex marriage will become an even more highly charged political lightning rod.

Multiple Masks

Today's teenagers often have more than one screen name to compartmentalize their online lives. They may use one screen name for instant messaging friends and another screen name for when they don't want friends to know they are online. Teenagers routinely try on different identities to see what fits and feels comfortably authentic. Some teenagers try on new identities every few months, especially since the Internet has made it so easy to do so.[4] A popular computer game like *The Sims*, for instance, allows young players to create and assume multiple identities in a simulated town.

Reinventing oneself is an American ideal, personified by Benjamin Franklin's continual forging of new identities (see chapter 7). Identity experimentation has now shifted to the Internet and is not confined just to teenagers. Imagine, for example, the increasingly common scenario of a young man who participates in online gaming with a screen name like *slamdunk*, who then goes into a chat room to discuss tattoos with a different screen name of *tatdude*, and who then finally changes into nice, clean screen-name clothes to instant message a girlfriend as *imthe14u*.

The public mask disguising the private self will become a growing conflict. Consumer items that enable one to become another person, to put on a public mask for an evening or a weekend, will become popular. Masques—worn at masked balls—will gain in popularity. As Pluto moves into Capricorn in 2008, we will see more and more masks; we just need to learn how to look for them. They could be party masks, surgical quarantine masks, or terrorists' kaffiyehs.

"Who's There?" Electronic Masks

Pretend personas will become commonplace as Pluto begins to move into Capricorn in 2008. Identity theft will be rampant; it's already bad, but it will intensify, becoming more pervasive and complex. Most identity theft is for financial gain and is related to computer databases. An employee or outsider gains access to Social Security numbers or credit card numbers and sells this information to criminals who then use the information to begin making purchases and applying for loans.

Any device that will enable someone to unlock or keep personal secrets will become valuable. Data privacy issues will be fought over in courtrooms, boardrooms, and bedrooms throughout Pluto's transit of Capricorn. It will be so easy to slip out of one identity and into another that quick, personal, surreptitious, and secure background checks will become invaluable.

Today, it has become easy to "google" a person—that is, to type an individual's name into an Internet search engine and discover private information about that person, from small online family photo albums to lawsuits. Access to personal information will continue to grow as Pluto enters Capricorn, and with it will come companies specializing in "un-googling"—expunging our private lives that have been made public. Protecting privacy will mean protecting our private lives that are becoming open books for anyone to check out and read.

Identity masks are already being made available. A new phone service will allow users to choose a fake phone number to fool caller ID software. Someone could get my employer's phone number, use it as a phone "mask," and call me. Of course I'll pick up the phone when I see my employer's phone number flash on the caller ID screen. These fake phone numbers are now available for a minimal fee.[5]

Other identity masks are also becoming available. E-mail inboxes abound with innocent-looking subject and sender masks that turn out to be X-rated come-ons or computer viruses. What if an individual has a less than stellar résumé—bankruptcy, child support liens, multiple divorces, maybe a prison sentence? People will be happy to purchase—or just steal—new personal histories in the name of romance or a new job. It's become so easy to masquerade as someone else, to hide our private selves behind a good public mask, that dating services now promote their unmasking ability: a pop-up ad for an Internet dating service promises thorough background checks to weed out felons and married people.

Life Galleries

Capricorn's preservation of the past will manifest through individual online "life galleries." Individuals are already beginning to collect and digitally store as much of their lives as possible. From photos to blogs to music, the computer can display our lives. Some camera-phone manufacturers encourage users to record their daily lives and turn the results into digital movies. When Pluto enters Capricorn, this phenomenon will lead to the creation of personal web museums and libraries.

It will also lead to a new type of identity theft. People who have innocently placed their lives online will find that somebody else has claimed that life—which has no copyright—as his or her own. This life theft will be done in order to impress someone, plagiarize, or sweeten a résumé.

In the movie *One Hour Photo,* a loner played by Robin Williams buys an old black-and-white, wallet-size picture of a woman. Hungry for acceptance and normality, he later pretends the picture is of his own mother. This sad vignette will become common in the future online world. One of the qualities of Saturn is loneliness, the dark shadow of solitude and introspection. During Pluto's journey through Saturn-ruled Capricorn, loneliness will fuel a rise in low-level identity theft.

Paying a Psychological Price

Although the ability to keep secrets is part of healthy social development, there is a psychological and emotional price to be paid for wearing a mask of concealment. It can be mentally exhausting to keep wearing a mask when the secret is a marital affair or a pornography addiction. When someone has too many secret identities or feels it necessary to hide from others behind a mask, the consequences can be shattering. For example, a person who lives a double life—responsible and conservative executive by day and secret seeker of illicit thrills by night—pays a price. It takes a lot of energy to keep a dark secret and maintain a part of the psyche that is separate.

When Pluto goes into Capricorn, we will experience this stress on a mass scale. The collective psyche will shudder under the weight of too much compartmentalizing and too little care for the integration of different parts of the social psyche. Many individuals will also experience this dissonance, especially with the availability of quick and furtive Internet disguises.

Capricorn is in the middle of the matrix where public meets private. Pluto will expose whatever is there. When individuals hear only the siren call of public expectations, they may become deaf to the cries of their own private needs. This can happen on a mass scale when a culture becomes so absorbed in meeting the expectations of others that it fails to heed its own inner, natural direction.

Nostalgia

Capricorn beckons us to revisit the past. It is one way that Capricorn tries to maintain the status quo.

Capricorn nostalgia is about to overwhelm us. Starting in 2008 or a little before, as Pluto approaches the cusp of Capricorn, advertising will make us ache with yearning for a past golden age of surf cars with side wood paneling, bread delivery trucks, milk in glass bottles, and just about anything that can be repackaged and sold as new. EBay bric-a-brac and 1970s-music CD infomercials are just the tip of this iceberg.

Nostalgia is one way to escape the reality of a dark present. Former President Ronald Reagan's 2004 death and funeral showed the depth of this public yearning. Capricorn has a tendency to mythologize the past. A nostalgic trip to the past, however, can be a lot more complicated than it seems. Margaret Atwood's *The Handmaid's Tale* is a haunting feminist novel set in an imaginary future when women serve as reproductive "handmaids." The narrator, one of the handmaids, observes "a rug on the floor, oval, of braided rags. This is the kind of touch [men] like: folk art, archaic, made by women, in their spare time, from things that have no further use. A return to traditional values."[6]

The problem with nostalgia and returning to a past "golden age" is that it may represent more than a simple love of old movies, posters, and music. It might mean turning back the clock on a whole host of social changes. Saturnine tradition might sound good if it just remains in a nice CD box set of 1970s music. But it could get packaged as a set of old-fashioned traditional moral values imposed by law.

The Masking of Power

Muhammad Ali, a Sun in Capricorn, was a master of masks. Capricorn has to do with wisdom and experience, as well as masks, and Muhammad Ali demonstrated the power of brains over brawn when he fought George Foreman in Zaire in 1974. Ali used a special technique to overcome the disadvantages of his aging legs and slower speed: he backed up against the ropes of the ring, covered his face with his gloves, and allowed Foreman to hammer him with body blows for seven rounds (a trick that came to be known as the "rope-a-dope" technique). Even Ali's own corner men were alarmed, begging him to get off the ropes and start fighting. Finally, Foreman grew fatigued from all the effort he had expended in hitting his opponent. Ali, however, having conserved his energy, suddenly began punching furiously and knocked Foreman out in the eighth round. The ability to transform a weakness (in Ali's case, age and relative slowness in the ring) into a strength (let the opponent, who is trained to be a punching machine, tire himself out until *he* becomes slower and weaker) is really winning by using brains over brawn, one of the positive attributes of a Capricorn.[7] Muhammad Ali showed how wearing a mask—in his case, of weakness in the ring—could be part of a strategy leading to victory. The masking of power and the use of clever strategies to conceal a winning hand will manifest in international relations and world conflict when Pluto is in Capricorn.

Astro-Connections Activity

Planets in the Movies

Next time you see a movie, filter it through Pluto (or Neptune). Do the themes, characters, costumes, mood, and tone seem to reflect Plutonian imagery? Movies that have a major impact—that get people talking about the themes and ideas behind the movie—always have a deeper social and cultural meaning and are reflective of Pluto's (and frequently Neptune's) passage through signs. What is that deeper symbolic meaning that can be unlocked through astrology? Can Pluto in Sagittarius help to unlock that meaning? Or is the film already beginning to show the next phase, Pluto in Capricorn? Popular entertainment appears superficial, but underneath the surface is a world of meaning that astrology can help us to understand.

Endnotes

1. Nathaniel Hawthorne, *The House of the Seven Gables* (New York: Dodd, Mead, and Company, 1979), 239.
2. "Steve Garvey," thebaseballpage.com, http://www.thebaseballpage.com/players/garvest01.php (accessed 23 August 2006).
3. Steven Forrest, *The Inner Sky: The Dynamic New Astrology for Everyone* (San Diego, California: ACS Publications, 1989), 82.
4. A recent study concluded that 56 percent of online teens in the U.S. have more than one e-mail address or screen name and most use different screen names or e-mail addresses to compartmentalize different parts of their lives online, enabling them to experiment with different personas. Of those teens with multiple addresses, nearly one quarter say that at least one of those addresses is a secret address that they use when they do not want their friends to know they are online. Source: "Internet and American Life: Teens and Their Friends," http://www.familyresource.com/lifestyles/technology/internet-and-american-life-teens-and-their-friends (accessed 23 August 2006).
5. Ken Belsen, "A Commercial Software Service Aims to Outfox Caller ID," *The New York Times*, 2 September 2004: C1.
6. Margaret Atwood, *The Handmaid's Tale* (Boston, Massachusetts: Houghton Mifflin Company, 1998), 7.
7. The illustration of Muhammad Ali's fighting prowess originally appeared in an article I wrote for the Feb./Mar. 2001 issue of *The Mountain Astrologer*. The article was titled "Mercury and the Transformational Sixth House."

CHAPTER 7

Ben Goes Electric: Inventing the Future

He poked fun at the rich and powerful and was one of the most acclaimed humorists of his time. He kept a revolution down to earth and practiced diplomatic networking on a global scale. He was curious and inventive, yet was always mindful of what was practical.

He was Benjamin Franklin, Capricorn extraordinaire, forever linked astrologically with the identity of the nation he helped found.

Pluto in Capricorn: Astrology Background

While the United States was officially declaring its independence from Great Britain, transiting Pluto was exactly conjoining Franklin's Capricorn Sun.

Benjamin Franklin exemplified an important side of Capricorn—the self-made individual who succeeds by virtue of hard work, networking, and keeping his nose to the grindstone. Benjamin Franklin's life seemed to demonstrate that through hard work and education, anyone could become prosperous in America. He is the forefather of writer Horatio Alger's success stories, as well as many of the modern business sagas that inspire readers to dream of great prosperity. Benjamin Franklin is the patron saint of the middle class and the small-business owner. These are two groups that will soon see great change. Between 2008 and 2024, during Pluto's passage through Capricorn, the middle economic class will experience an intense and wrenching transformation.

Franklin personifies the all-American success story, a stature that has been inflated over the centuries to almost mythic proportions. Franklin was in fact a much more complex figure than he appears, coming to us through the haze of history. Although for many he symbolizes the nation's up-from-the-bootstraps potential, Franklin exemplifies for others the crass materialistic acquiring and spending of a new nation.[1] These are two sides of Capricorn that will soon find strong expression in American culture—and cause society to re-examine the meaning of success. An already-visible trend is dressing down or, conversely, displaying false affectations of wealth. The rich will dress like factory workers and drive pickup trucks to show their supposed working-class roots, while others of lesser means will go into overwhelming debt to purchase Cadillac Escalades.

When Pluto goes into Capricorn, people will question and debate the true meaning of success. The American conflict over the meaning and display of wealth is a theme that runs from *The Great Gatsby* to *The Godfather*. Benjamin Franklin's rags-to-riches mythology led to the fictional excesses of Jay Gatsby and Vito Corleone. In F. Scott Fitzgerald's novel, Jay Gatsby strives to become a self-made millionaire in order to win the love of Daisy Buchanan. Fitzgerald, the author, even has Gatsby make a daily schedule that bears a striking resemblance to Ben Franklin's virtuous self-improvement plan. In Franklin's plan, described in his *Autobiography,* he devoted time to "Examination of the Day." He listed thirteen virtues, such as temperance and industry, then set about systematically charting his development of each.[2] Gatsby's similar attempts to achieve the American Dream turn him into a robotic To Do checklist.

In *The Godfather,* Don Vito Corleone also pursues the American Dream, networking his way to wealth, success, and influence. Although he is the head of a Mafia "family," Vito Corleone has built a respectable life on Long Island. In many ways, he has achieved the immigrant American Dream. He has nice cars, a beautiful home, and a better life for his children—especially younger son Michael, who seems untainted by the family's Mafia business.

In the famous movie sequel, *The Godfather: Part II,* Michael Corleone reveals the true dark side of the pursuit of the American Dream. Inheriting his father's Mob business, he lives a life of eminent outward respectability and enviable achievement, but it is a life bought and maintained with ruthless murder and blackmail. He is driven by many of the character traits we most admire in society, qualities that can shine in a Capricorn. Michael Corleone is detached, tough-minded, and practical. He gets things done. Pluto in Capricorn may not bring out the American gangster, but sometimes people cut corners in order to achieve goals—and Capricorn is very much about getting "there," wherever there might be.

This chapter will look at how the traditional values of Capricorn will play out in the broader culture when Pluto enters the sign of the sure-footed goat. Some "Ben Franklin trends" for Pluto in Capricorn:

- The world will be networked as never before.
- Philanthropy and compassion will make a comeback.
- Restraint will be a key to the coming age.
- Astrophysics will lead to new discoveries that will alter the meaning of time.
- More television shows and movies will center around themes of death and dying.
- Fashion will reflect the influence of Capricorn. Cold-weather clothing will become fashionable—or a necessity because of climate change.
- The loneliness of an aging population will make itself felt in places of worship and senior citizen dating services.
- Sure-footed team leaders in any field who are able to render split-second decisions will be admired and rewarded.
- In-your-face comedians will be replaced by humorists who gently mock the powerful and elite.

Ambition and Networking

Benjamin Franklin was a consummate networker. One of the traits of Capricorn is a strong desire to get ahead by networking one's way to the top, like the mountain goat leaping from one toehold to the next. This type of ambition can take many forms. Sometimes it can manifest as behind-the-scenes manipulation to get one's way. At other times, it can be hobnobbing with those more important and powerful than oneself in order to shine by reflection.

A television network is created by local stations linked to form a single broadcast entity. When it grows and becomes big, such a network can become powerful. When Pluto goes into Capricorn, a number of corporate, governmental, and international networks will wield considerable power. There will be fewer checks and balances. A problem with this type of power structure is that there are disenfranchised people on the bottom who become angry at being left out.

When Pluto was in Capricorn during the 1700s, British authority in America formed a network of control, governing everything from colonial expansion to trade. This network was challenged by disenfranchised American colonists. A feeling of political impotence led to the Boston Tea Party, in which a group of American colonists protested the import of British tea by throwing it overboard in Boston Harbor. When Pluto moves into Capricorn, we may see similar protests and rebellions by those who feel left out of the power structure.

On the other hand, Capricorn the mountain goat is able to bound from crag to rocky crag and never stumble. Business managers, executives, or leaders in any field who can exhibit sure-footedness will be rewarded. They will be renowned for nimble footwork, unlike the buffed and steroid-fed athletes of Pluto in Sagittarius. Team players who scan the field and render split-second decisions will achieve a new measure of respect and reward.

Philanthropy and Compassion

One outcome of the coming cultural debate about the meaning of success will be greater charity. Capricorn can manifest as charitable public and community service. Benjamin Franklin devoted a considerable portion of his life to philanthropy and was more concerned with giving than with getting. He retired at age forty-two, devoting the rest of a long life to serving his community and nation. This sense of altruistic duty is one of the higher potentials of Capricorn and will become more prevalent when Pluto moves into Capricorn. Humanitarian Clara Barton, founder of the American Red Cross (see the Uranus-Neptune Profile at the end of chapter 10), was a Capricorn who represented the charitable expression of this sign.

The possibility of greater modesty, self-effacement, and compassion in the coming years is exemplified by another Sun in Capricorn, Saint Thérèse de Lisieux. Known as the "mystic of the ordinary," she was a nineteenth-century Carmelite nun who entered her order as a teenager and died young, at the age of twenty-four, from tuberculosis. She wrote *The Story of a Soul,* which tells of her efforts to turn small acts of human service into acts of divine devotion. She created a special devotional technique she called the "little way," which involved humility, service, and spiritual growth employed in everyday, mundane tasks. A nun whose personal habits irritated her, for instance, became an opportunity to learn greater patience and tolerance.

It may appear contradictory to say that Pluto in Capricorn will result in an uninhibited cultural party atmosphere (see chapter 5) *and* greater modesty. However, society and culture are never simple and the sign of Capricorn is itself ambivalent, reaching for both the heights and the depths.

The Mask of Self-Restraint

As discussed in chapter 6, masked identities will be a powerful trend surfacing in culture when Pluto moves into Capricorn. Franklin had many masks. He wrote using pseudonyms for many years, before the publication of his *Autobiography,* under the guises of Silence Dogood, Polly Baker, and many others. In fact, he used forty-two various pseudonyms. His most famous pen name was Richard Saunders, the supposed author of *Poor Richard's Almanack.*

Just as Ben Franklin was adept at creating a persona to fit the occasion or the issue, Capricorn excels at never being too revealing. It holds back just enough to maintain distance and reticence. When change is required, Capricorn is ready and able, like the agile mountain goat, to step nimbly into the next public role.

Restraint will be a key quality as Pluto moves into Capricorn. "Poor Richard" wrote in his almanac that one should "let all men know thee, but no man know thee thoroughly: Men freely ford that see the shallows."[3] In other words, seeming deep and reserved was preferable to "letting it all hang out." However, keeping certain compartments of the human psyche hidden can lead to secretiveness and deception. The Internet and blogs have made it extremely easy to let everyone in on a blogger's life while letting no one see the true inner self. As pointed out in the previous chapter, it takes a lot of emotional energy to keep the psyche under wraps.

Restraint can also be projected onto others in the form of imprisonment, trade restraints, restraining other nations, restraining orders, and so forth. As noted in chapter 5, repression can be one outcome of Pluto in Capricorn.

Time and Aging

The ruler of Capricorn, Saturn, is the planet of time. When Pluto enters Capricorn, our conception of time will be transformed. Astrophysics may lead to the

Saturn and Osteoporosis

Saturn governs old age. It also rules bones, the body's skeletal support structure. When Pluto enters Capricorn, we will see problems in this area. Osteoporosis is a weakening of the bone structure, causing the bones to become brittle and more prone to fracture. It is a disease most often associated with aging. Just as diabetes became a silent epidemic during Pluto's transit through Sagittarius, osteoporosis will reach epidemic proportions with Pluto's entry into Capricorn.

discovery of time distortions. A new understanding of the shape of the universe may alter our sense of what time is. Then again, the passage of time might really get speeded up; we could have a number of fast-moving events hit us and make time race by.

When Pluto, the astrological symbol of death, goes from happy-go-lucky Sagittarius into sober Capricorn, it will mark a tremendous change. In order for change to occur, something has to die. Accompanying radical change are forms of death imagery which percolate up from the collective psyche.[4] We can expect this imagery to surface in unusual ways that could be either entertaining or deeply disturbing and emotional.

Funerals will take on an aura of pomp and circumstance. They will also become more personal and less traditional as the individualistic Pluto in Leo generation begins to pass away. Former U.S. President Ronald Reagan's 2004 funeral carried overtones of the passing of an age. It could serve as a template for future funerals as the political and cultural leaders of an older era die, leaving the nation and world aching for the golden, tranquil past.

More television comedies will center around death and dying. Death has been a central fixture of humor for centuries, but more than ever we will find ourselves whistling—and giggling—past the graveyard.

Capricorn symbolizes loneliness. To combat this, people will be seeking connections, either personal or spiritual. The loneliness of an aging population will make itself felt in churches and in senior citizen dating services.

Capricorn Clothing

Because Capricorn is a hardworking sign, clothing styles will be designed for work. Expect clothing to be utilitarian. Business suits might not seem utilitarian but they mark someone as belonging to the world of business. Suits are professional attire. Gone will be the colorful Sagittarian Jerry Garcia neckties and in will come thin, sleek satin neckties in dark colors. Women's clothing will reflect the working world.

Beige khakis and denim work shirts will be popular.

Winter clothes will also become more prevalent, due perhaps to the vagaries of fashion or climate change. Mountaineering clothing styles will be popular. There will be a fashion trend favoring hooded parkas, mittens, and snow boots.

The mountain-goat agility of Capricorn will be reflected in footwear. The popular Sherpa-style Ugg boots will continue to evolve. Rock-climbing shoes will become popular.

Dark, natural fabrics and loose clothing of the type worn to a yoga class will become more prevalent.

Capricorn Humor

Capricorn has a surprising amount of frivolity. Among his many accomplishments, Ben Franklin was also a folksy humorist who enjoyed poking adroit fun at others. Franklin's *Poor Richard's Almanack* was more than just a collection of short nostrums and adages. It was also a humor book. Adapting the pen name of Richard Saunders gave Franklin freedom to express his thoughts with more dramatic license. Poor Richard's innocent persona allowed him to poke fun at young America's rich and powerful elite.[5]

Comedian Steve Allen cultivated a wry, urbane image, perfectly displaying the type of Capricorn humor we can expect to see more of as Pluto edges into Capricorn. His Capricorn Sun showcased a droll, edgy sense of humor suited for late-night television. He began *The Tonight Show* in 1953 and later hosted the prime-time *Steve Allen Show*, where he developed the man on the street interview with Don Knotts, Tom Poston, and others. In keeping with his Capricorn nature, Steve Allen was very concerned with television's image and decried what he felt were the corrosive excesses of violence and sex on television.

Astro-Connections Activity

Bestseller Lists

Look at the top ten best-selling books on Amazon.com, or on any national bestseller list. If you're not already familiar with some of the books, you can read descriptions on the Internet. Then, look at the keywords list for the sign Pluto is currently passing through: either Sagittarius or Capricorn. Note keywords that match the books. Can you see any patterns emerging?

Endnotes

1. Gordon Woods, *The Americanization of Benjamin Franklin* (New York: The Penguin Press, 2004), 5.
2. Benjamin Franklin, *The Autobiography and Other Writings of Benjamin Franklin* (New York: Dodd, Mead, & Company, 1963), 90–96.
3. Benjamin Franklin, *Poor Richard's Almanack,* 1743, reproduced online at "Documents for the Study of American History," http://www.vlib.us/amdocs/texts/prichard43.html (accessed 23 August 2006).
4. Liz Greene, *The Outer Planets and Their Cycles: The Astrology of the Collective* (Sebastopol, California: CRCS Publications, 1996) 10. Greene is referring to the individual, but these words might also apply to the collective.
5. Walter Isaacson, "The Amazing Adventures of Ben Franklin: Citizen Ben's Great Virtues" *Time* online edition, 7 July 2003, http://www.time.com/time/2003/franklin/bffranklin3.html (accessed 22 August 2006).

PART III

Coming Attractions with Uranus and Neptune

Uranus and Neptune are having a powerful impact on our world. Seldom have these two planets been as symbolically linked as they are now. The Uranus-Neptune conjunction of 1993 was followed a short decade later by these two planets "trading signs." The intensified merging and sharing of Uranus and Neptune is affecting social and cultural trends everywhere.

CHAPTER 8

The Dreaming Planet: Neptune

NEPTUNE IS. . .

Idealized
Visionary
Fashion
Drugs
Merging
Worship
Ephemeral
Glamorous
Imagination
Transcendence
Yearning
Dissolving

Neptune Background

From the distance of Voyager 2, Neptune is the color of blue denim, an effect resulting from surface methane. Neptune is considered by astronomers to be a "gas giant." The outer third of the planet is composed of heated gases and, in fact, astrological Neptune rules gas. Neptune takes 165 years to orbit the sun, spending almost fourteen years in each zodiac sign and, like Pluto, it marks the passage of a generation.

Astrologers place a great deal of significance on events that occurred when Uranus, Neptune, and Pluto were discovered, believing that such events indicate what they rule. Neptune's discovery in 1846 coincided with early developments in photography, genetics, and medicine—especially anesthesia with its ability to numb the senses. The sewing machine was invented in the same year that Neptune was discovered, and Neptune is closely linked to fashion and dress. Spiritualism, American Transcendentalism, and general interest in the spirit world blossomed at the time of Neptune's discovery. The gothic novel *Jane Eyre* was also published.

Important Ways Neptune Affects Us

- Neptune is glamour and what we glamorize.
- Neptune is associated with fashion and marketing.
- Neptune rules movies, celebrities, and popular entertainment that capture the public's imagination and fancy.
- Neptune is associated with collective dreams and yearnings for extraordinary experiences. It rules a culture's quasi-mystical aspirations and illusive quests.
- Neptune is transcendent unity.

Glamorous Images

Neptune is one of the most important planets affecting the modern world. Anytime we walk through the supermarket checkout line, we see this watery planet—where it is called the *Star, People* magazine, or *The National Enquirer*. Neptune is the planet of celebrity, movies, unaccountable fashion waves, and marketing. Neptune reflects and glitters. It is the gleam in the eye of the public, caught and refracted in a retailing prism. Neptune gilds popularity with a platinum sheen.

It rules the sea, and Neptunian cultural phenomena appear like sunlight shimmering on the magical surface of the ocean.

The word "glamour" has its linguistic roots in the idea of casting a spell or using magical power to influence others, and this idea is close to the hypnotic, Neptunian quality of modern glamour.

One has only to look at the public and media fascination with pop singer Britney Spears or at that 1950s embodiment of feminine glamour and allure, Marilyn Monroe. Both have Neptune powerfully accented in their horoscopes. Each cast a spell over the public, as if they had scattered handfuls of Neptunian glitter dust over their audiences. Britney Spears's music videos brought new meaning to the phrase "sex appeal," and even President Kennedy appeared mesmerized by Marilyn Monroe's throaty rendition of "Happy Birthday."

Britney Spears and Marilyn Monroe: Astrology Background

Britney Spears has four planets, including Neptune, in fiery Sagittarius. Marilyn Monroe has Neptune in her First House—always a powerful placement in a horoscope—forming part of a T-square with Jupiter and Saturn.

Neptunian glamour is a powerful image that can captivate the public, but it is not necessarily real. Marilyn Monroe projected the film persona of a sexy, addle-brained blonde, but that wasn't the real Marilyn Monroe: she was in fact an intelligent woman married to the playwright who gave us *Death of a Salesman*.

Brad Pitt's sexy, charismatic Neptune in Scorpio has helped to give him a similar hypnotic hold. Neptune transcends boundaries, and this male sex symbol is a star whose Neptunian appeal seemingly knows no bounds. In a similar vein, Neptune in Leo Paul Newman has cast a soothing and charismatic spell over worldwide movie audiences of both sexes for five decades.

Fashion and Marketing

Neptune is at the intersection of marketing, fashion, and popular entertainment. This meeting point may be seen in many popular movies. For example, the 1983 movie *Flashdance* was about a female welder who worked a second job as an exotic dancer. Her dream was to become a ballet dancer. The movie was panned by critics for its implausible juxtaposition of blue-collar arc welding and highbrow classical dancing. However, the movie featured an inexhaustible soundtrack of number-one songs that elevated the film into 1980s iconic status—and served as a template for future movie marketers. It also spawned a fashion look for twenty- and thirty-something young women. Off-the-shoulder sweatshirts and leg warmers became ubiquitous, and—even better—one didn't need to be working out at a dance studio to wear them.

Fashion and Neptune have a great deal in common. Both are ephemeral and elusive. In many ways, fashion *is* Neptune. If fashion symbolizes cultural patterns, then the astrology of fashion should tell us about broader changes in the culture.

Neptune and Blue Jeans

Denim is one example of how the astrology of fashion reveals a broader cultural transformation.

Television commercials for blue jeans contain deep emotional symbols, demonstrating that blue jeans stand for a lot more than just sturdy leg wear. In an essay on the evolution of blue jeans, Beverly Gordon wrote: "Changes in jean styling, embellishment, and marketing are closely tied to changes in society as a whole, and these changes serve as a subtle but accurate barometer of trends in contemporary popular culture."[1]

Blue jeans made their first appearance in the latter part of the nineteenth century while **Neptune was in Taurus.**[2] Taurus is an earth sign, symbolizing the land, stamina, and agriculture. The first blue jeans had strong rivets at the stress points. Early blue jeans were not meant to be a fashion statement, but rather were seen as sturdy, wearable clothing on the farm and on the Wild West frontier.

When **Neptune entered Gemini**, jeans multiplied. Sears Roebuck began offering several different styles of blue jeans. Levi's competed with Wrangler.

With **Neptune in Leo**—the sign of the individual and creative expression—in the 1920s, blue jeans became a statement of

continued . . .

Neptune in Scorpio and the Beatles

Neptune was in the Pluto-ruled water sign of Scorpio during the 1960s. The famous transformation of the Beatles from leather-jacketed ruffians to mop-topped and mod-clothed teen idols who appeared on *The Ed Sullivan Show* illustrated Neptune's powerful ability to sweep through the culture.

It also showed how Neptune can bring out the qualities of an astrological sign through music. Scorpio has to do with depth, darkness, and hidden emotions. The Beatles, for a time, owned the world through music and image. Beatles manager Brian Epstein took "the youngsters"—as Ed Sullivan called them—and transformed them from tough Liverpool teens into cute scrub-faced idols wearing suits and ties. The Beatles still managed to retain a hint of Scorpio menace, but they were packaged in hip, slick, and cool Neptune vinyl. They completed their Neptune in Scorpio cultural journey with a visit to Maharishi Mahesh Yogi, with whom they posed in paisley-and-incense splendor.

Roadside Memorials

A young man is shot and killed while standing on a street corner with friends. On the grass border between the sidewalk and the street, next to a street sign and marking the spot where he died, a simple memorial appears. It consists of fresh flowers, votive candles, and a small wooden cross.

A local teenage girl out jogging with her father is struck and killed by an automobile. A roadside memorial is erected. This one has flowers, a small, red Mylar heart balloon, and a pinwheel.

Roadside memorials, long a fixture in New Mexico where they are called *descansos* (resting places), have become common in other states and countries. The randomness of these roadside memorials is unsettling, a reminder that sudden death is never far away. Although Pluto is often associated with death, Neptune is a planet of bonding on a transcendent level.

With the gentle connection of a simple roadside memorial, we share in the grief of strangers. This is the power of Neptune. It is where we merge, connected and borderless.

Deep emotional bonding with strangers often requires the force of a tragedy. How often have we heard others say, in the aftermath of a personal tragedy, that the good that came out of misfortune was realizing how much others cared?

individual expression. An artists' colony in Santa Fe, New Mexico, for example, adopted blue jeans as a way of saying, "We are different."

When **Neptune was in service-oriented Virgo** during World War II, jeans were worn in the factory. They became identified with the patriotic effort to win the war. There was a feeling of service and unity associated with jeans.

In the 1960s, when **Neptune was in Scorpio**, blue jeans became an anti-fashion statement, de rigueur apparel for counterculture youth.

Neptune in sartorial Sagittarius in the 1970s and early 1980s gave us the first designer jeans. Denim went high couture.

In 1995, while **Neptune was in Capricorn**, IBM stopped requiring its employees to wear business suits. Blue jeans became part of the corporate sphere on casual Fridays, and were a Capricorn fashion statement at work: "I am a working guy or gal." As astrologer Liz Greene points out, during Neptune in Capricorn, blue jeans also had a touch of nostalgia for the vanished past of the Wild West.[3]

When **Neptune entered the air sign Aquarius** in 1998, blue jeans became loose and baggy—filled with more air than leg. They were unconventional, worn by hip-hop performers and adopted as quirky youth attire.

Neptune and the U.S. Horoscope: Astrology Background

In 2010, transiting Neptune will go over the Moon in the U.S. horoscope. The Moon traditionally represents the people of a nation. As noted in the Astrology Background on page 36, stressful planetary aspects affecting our sense of national security will develop in 2010. The fact that transiting Neptune will be conjoining the U.S. Moon at the same time indicates that emotional bonding will take place on a mass level.

Pisces—Merging and Transcendence

There are two ways of spreading light: to be
The candle or the mirror that reflects it.
—Edith Wharton, "Vesalius in Zante"

Neptune can suggest the public desire for transcendent experiences. Because Neptune rules the sea, it also relates to the unconscious. Certain events and popular entertainment can, whether by accident or design, tap the hidden depths of a culture's unconscious yearning.

Neptune rules Pisces, the twelfth sign of the zodiac and the culmination of a cycle. Pisces can be otherworldly and spiritual or just escapist. It can be compassionate and artistic or lonely and confused. It relates to the collective unconscious. Famous people with the Sun in Pisces are often like perfectly still ponds reflecting the public face peering into the surfaces. Sun in Pisces Ansel Adams was renowned for his black-and-white photographs of Yosemite's "Moon and Half Dome" or "Moonrise, Hernandez, New Mexico." His photos are perfect Piscean reflections.

Fred Rogers: Astrology Background

Mister Rogers had four planets in Pisces: the Sun, Moon, Mercury, and Venus.

Neptune is not just about celebrities. As the ruler of Pisces, Neptune also shows a compassionate, spiritual side. Fred Rogers—or Mister Rogers, as he was known to generations of toddlers—is a perfect example. Fred Rogers's Sun formed part of a powerful Pisces pattern in his horoscope.

On his television show, *Mister Rogers' Neighborhood*, he merged with his young audience by exuding a soothing and slow-paced childlike consciousness. His daily sign-off included the reassurance, "People *can* like you *just* the way you are." Many adults have cherished memories of watching Mister Rogers with their own children.

Prior to Neptune's discovery, the traditional ruler of Pisces was Jupiter. One can see in a Pisces Sun like Fred Rogers the expansive and spiritual qualities of Jupiter, seeking to transcend boundaries of time and space. Fred Rogers would occasionally visit college campuses as a guest speaker. The jaded college crowd would stand and applaud, many with tears in their eyes as they recalled his tranquil presence in their own childhoods. Neptune-ruled Pisces can awaken in us a deep awareness of transcendent unity.

Fred Rogers was an ordained Presbyterian minister who was given the mission of carrying a Christian message to children. He never used his religion as a weapon or brandished it in anger. Instead, he preached the Neptunian virtues of compassion, love, and tolerance.

Neptune and Disco

Picture one of those mirrored disco balls turning, reflecting the shimmering club lights. The club vibrates with pulsating, ephemeral music in a sea of flowing, swirling shirts and dresses. Disco, a fashion and music trend which captured the public imagination in the 1970s, was Neptunian. Disco also originated in clubs where dancing was fueled by drugs and alcohol, both of which relate to Neptune.

Throughout the 1970s, Neptune was in Sagittarius, the sign of the centaur archer: young people donned white suits and disco dresses, adopting the quintessential Neptune in Sagittarius dance-floor pose made famous by John Travolta in *Saturday Night Fever*—one arm extended, finger pointing skyward. Neptune is fashion and one of the keywords for Sagittarius is expansion, so during this time we had "fashion expansion"—platform shoes, broad padded shoulders, and Elton John's oversize sunglasses.

Neptune Profile: Stevie Nicks

Stevie Nicks is an ethereal chanteuse and prolific songwriter. She is most famous for being the sultry-voiced singer with the long platinum blonde hair, china-doll complexion, and black chiffon dress in the 1970s rock group Fleetwood Mac. Her music has transcended boundaries, appealing to women as well as to men. Her songs are links in a Neptune chain that connects her audience to dreams of life and love. In many ways, she is an embodiment of Neptune, a planet that exerts a very strong influence in her horoscope.

She achieved superstardom in 1977 with the release of the Fleetwood Mac album *Rumours*. This album, along with Fleetwood Mac's earlier self-titled album, included songs whose popularity has endured up until the present, including "Rhiannon," about a flying witch, and "Dreams." Stevie Nicks brought a mesmerizing beauty to the maligned music of the 1970s. She has also released best-selling solo albums, such as *Bella Donna* and *Trouble in Shangri-La*.

Stevie Nicks's lyrics are very Neptunian. Songs such as "Silver Springs" employ the imagery of water and dreams, and "Dreams" includes Neptune-tinged verses.

One expression of a strong Neptune in the horoscope can be problems with drugs or alcohol, and Stevie Nicks has spoken publicly about how she has overcome addictions to cocaine and the tranquilizer Klonopin.

Stevie Nicks went from the thrift stores to high-priestess fashion icon. In the earliest stages of her career, her stage wear came from second-hand clothing stores. Today, she spends a great deal of money to maintain a stage wardrobe that projects the image for which she is known. Her gypsy fashion style is a true reflection of Neptune: black dresses accented with glittering shawls and brightly-colored seven-inch platform boots. Neptune, a planet associated with water, governs not only the flow of fashion but also the type of swirling dresses and accoutrements favored by Stevie Nicks.

Nicks casts a Neptunian spell over the audience during the ending to "Gold Dust Woman," as she slowly and hypnotically twirls in rapturous circles at the center of the stage, illuminated by a solo spotlight, gold shawl gently billowing, tambourine held aloft. It is like watching a tidal eddy in the moonlight, a transfixing Neptunian moment.

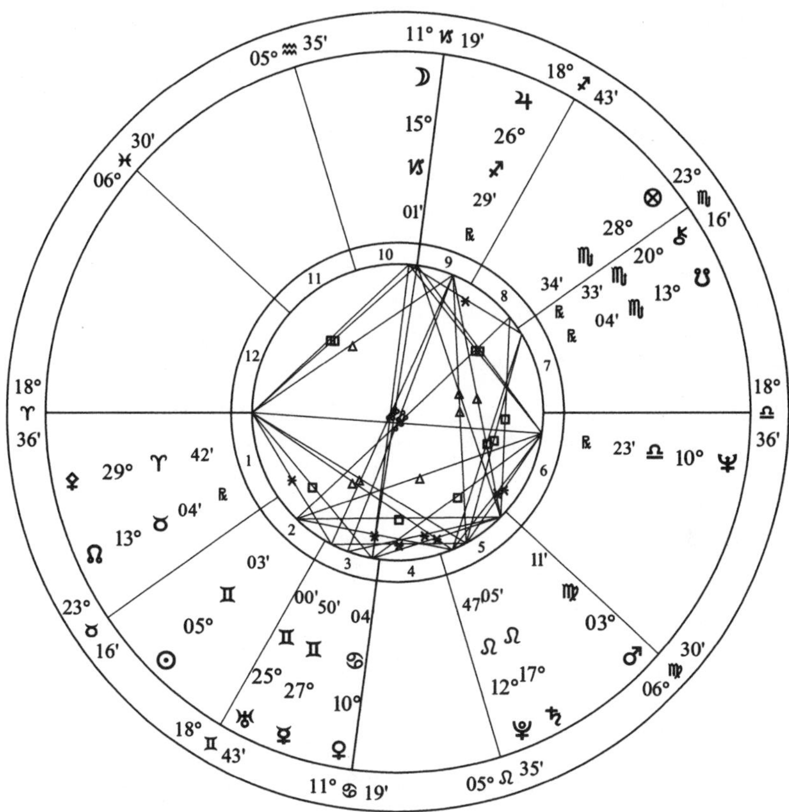

Stevie Nicks
May 26, 1948 / 3:02 AM MST
Phoenix, Arizona / Placidus houses

Stevie Nicks: Astrology Background

Stevie Nicks's Sixth House Neptune exactly squares her dreamy Venus in Cancer. Neptune also squares a hardworking and practical Moon in Capricorn. These two squares combine to form a T-square, with the energy of a stressed Neptune emptying into the Twelfth House, which just happens to have Pisces on the cusp in Nicks's horoscope—and Neptune rules Pisces. There is a lot of musically captivating power in this configuration, although it also symbolizes drug problems. The confluence of Neptune, Pisces, and the Twelfth House all add up to a very Neptunian persona.

There are several horoscope factors that have given Stevie Nicks survival strength in the difficult music business:

- Her Moon is in Capricorn in the Tenth House, giving her real staying power. She always stays focused on her work, career, and public persona—those are what nourish her.
- Her Ascendant is in fiery, get-it-done, full-speed-ahead Aries.
- Her Gemini Sun squares a creative and meticulous Fifth House Virgo Mars, allowing her to focus her musical energies and stay grounded.
- She has the asteroid Pallas Athena in her first house, giving it a strong emphasis in her life. Pallas Athena is the independent career woman and the fight to escape male domination.

Astro-Connections Activity

Trends Worksheet

This worksheet may be completed for Uranus, Neptune, or Pluto.

Circle one: Uranus Neptune Pluto

Current sign (see Appendix D): ______________________

Keyword combination (one planet keyword and one sign keyword):

______________________	______________________
Uranus, Neptune, or Pluto Keyword	Sign Keyword

List five famous modern people, places, or things that convey this keyword combination:

1.
2.
3.
4.
5.

What is a movie or TV show that embodies this keyword combination?

What is a clothing fashion that embodies this keyword combination?

Endnotes

1. Beverly Gordon, "American Denim: Blue Jeans and Their Multiple Layers of Meaning," *Dress and Popular Culture*, ed. Patricia A. Cunningham and Susan Voso Lab (Bowling Green, Ohio: Bowling Green State University Popular Press, 1991), 31. Some of the historical observations about blue jeans in this section are from Beverly Gordon's essay.
2. Liz Greene, *The Astrological Neptune and the Quest for Redemption* (York Beach, Maine: Samuel Weiser, 1996), 257.

CHAPTER 9

The Freedom Planet: Uranus

URANUS IS . . .

Quirky
Prophetic
Rebellious
Revolutionary
Explosive
Inventive
Objective
Technology
Utopian
Quickening
Projecting
Sudden awakening
Freedom

Uranus Background

Uranus is a slightly under-inflated, turquoise-colored beach ball. It does not have the nice, round, and globular shape of the other eight planets. In keeping with its nonconformist image, Uranus likes to be different.

As noted in chapter 8, important events that took place when an outer planet was discovered are indicative of that planet's basic nature. Uranus was discovered in 1781, a time of revolutionary ferment. However, both the American Revolution of 1776 and the French Revolution of 1789 brought forth democracies. These were different from various South American revolutions or the Communist revolution in Cuba. Real cultural revolutions are better understood in terms of the Uranus-Pluto conjunction (see chapter 14).

Uranus, the sky god in Greek myth, is the modern planetary ruler of Aquarius. Before the discovery of the planet Uranus, however, Aquarius had always been ruled by Saturn, a conservative planet. Saturn has to do with detachment and an unemotional nature, and Aquarius is imbued with some of these qualities. Symbolically, Aquarius bears water on its broad shoulders, pouring it down to a world thirsty for knowledge and awareness.

Aquarius is a fixed sign, meaning it does not change easily. Therefore, the egalitarian society (favoring equality of social classes) and revolutionary ideas associated with Aquarius tend to be stabilizing.

Six Cultural Areas Ruled by Uranus

Uranus influences several important areas of modern life:

- Uranus rules things that are in the air, including ideas, radio, and television.
- It has to do with secular prophets and visionaries.
- It is the eruption of a powerful idea.
- Uranus is technology and the control of nature.
- It is anti-fashion.
- Uranus is the cultural rebel.

In the Air

Aquarius has to do with the public airwaves: radio, TV, and the wireless Internet. It is also related to sudden mental insights and the world of thought. Uranus and Aquarius insights are brilliant flashes of lightning in the cultural sky. Bill Gates, the founder of Microsoft, has a powerful Uranus in his horoscope. When he was a teenager, his mother asked him why he wasn't busy. His irritated Uranian reply: "I'm thinking."[1]

Bill Gates: Astrology Background

Bill Gates has Uranus strongly positioned in his First House. When his horoscope is overlaid on the U.S. horoscope (a process of chart comparison called synastry), Gates's Ascendant is exactly on the U.S. Part of Fortune, a powerful placement, made even more remarkable by Gates's Second House Jupiter-Pluto conjunction opposing the U.S. Moon.

Ideas that are "in the air" are related to Uranus. Some individuals with a strong Uranus or Aquarius in their horoscopes can appear a bit airheaded. Uranus is not grounded unless it is in aspect to another planet that keeps it tethered to the ground. Uranus is like a helium balloon that can drift skyward unless it is held down. That is why many inventions and new ideas are Uranian—they have broken the cords that bind us to old ways of thinking and soared through clouds into the open sky.

Aquarius can show its Saturn side in some unusual ways. We like to think of Saturn as being very grounded and down-to-earth, but if someone has the Saturnine qualities of detachment and an unemotional nature they can be seen as kooky or unconventional. Two twentieth-century United States presidents, Franklin D. Roosevelt and Ronald Reagan, were Aquarius Suns who were able to emotionally detach from world events. Franklin Roosevelt and his wife, Eleanor, created an unconventional White House environment. In the midst of World War II's upheavals, FDR—the leader of the free world—could sometimes be found engrossed in his stamp collection.[2] Ronald Reagan delighted in retelling stories from his days as a movie actor, stopped work at five o'clock, and loved to catch his breath at his ranch, named Rancho del Cielo. The name means Heavenly Ranch, an appropriate name for an Aquarian retreat.

As a point of comparison, Capricorn Richard Nixon "relaxed" while strolling on the beach—wearing a dark business suit. Capricorn, which was discussed in detail in Part II, is also ruled by Saturn. In the case of Capricorn, however, Saturn expresses itself differently and Capricorn does not have a modern co-ruler like Aquarius.

Prophets and Visionaries

Uranus has to do with individuals who are able to envision the future. They often take an interest in reforming society. The novels of Aquarian Charles Dickens, for example, exposed aspects of Victorian society that needed to be changed.

Jules Verne, Betty Friedan, and Abraham Lincoln were Aquarius Suns. All three were prophetic or visionary. French science fiction novelist Jules Verne foresaw rocket journeys in *From the Earth to the Moon* and modern global travel in *Around the World in 80 Days*. Betty Friedan's *The Feminine Mystique* launched modern feminism. Abraham Lincoln's vision of a more perfect union rallied public support and his own sagging morale during the dark days of the Civil War.

When we look at Uranus and its relationship to culture today, it is important to notice those individuals who are envisioning the future. Uranus is an individualistic planet and, unlike the broad sweep of Pluto and Neptune, its widespread cultural influences are often driven by individuals who can see what many of us cannot yet discern.

Aquarius, a fixed sign, likes the air to be stable—no wind or upsetting weather conditions. Once the Uranian helium balloon has been released into the atmosphere, it does not like to be blown about with no sense of control. Microsoft's Bill Gates may be a visionary software developer, but he also controls ninety percent of the computer operating systems market.

The Sky's the Limit: Uranus in Aquarius

One of the best ways to understand both Uranus and Aquarius is to look at how some of the keyword combinations (see Appendix A) manifested during the transit of Uranus through Aquarius between 1996 and 2003. Uranus rules computers and many forms of modern technology. Aquarius is associated with the borderless Internet. While Uranus was in Aquarius, technology and the Internet exploded in an egalitarian revolution. Worldwide Internet use soared from under fifty million users in 1996 to over half a billion in 2002.

During this time, the world also experienced a sudden awakening—or quickening—of globalization. Uranus and Aquarius can both envision a utopian tomorrow, which is sometimes a future seen through rose-colored glasses. Thomas Friedman's *The Lexus and the Olive Tree* extolled a utopian world where countries are joined by a borderless world economy. Computers also gave rise to utopian ideals of a perfect digital world.

Like Aquarius, the Internet unifies, establishes community, breaks down borders, and ideally places users on a level playing field. The World Wide Web gives the individual a voice equal to that of rulers and institutions. It is revolutionary, democratizing power in ways we do not yet understand. At its base is the visionary utopian ideal of a better world where we are all freely connected. We can see the Internet's egalitarian essence in the way that it allows individuals a voice through weblogs (commonly known as blogs).

The Internet also signifies another Aquarian trait, the public domain—or what Lawrence Lessig refers to as the Commons, an area where we can all meet as equals to exchange information and discuss the issues of the day.[3] It is akin to the old-fashioned town meeting. Although the Internet was an egalitarian invention, it may not evolve as such. Along with opportunities for collective freedom, the Internet has also revealed freedom's downside—a parallel explosion in Internet pornography, junk e-mail, and fraud. Pluto's entry into Capricorn in 2008 will have serious repercussions in this area of the Internet (see chapter 4).

The explosive scope of the Internet's borderless world has created an intense conflict over peer-to-peer file sharing—free music and movie downloading. Peer-to-peer file participants make music and movies available to one another in an Aquarian open network. Napster, the music downloading company, was launched in 1997, shortly after Uranus went into Aquarius. At its peak, 2.7 billion files were downloaded in a single month. Peer-to-peer file sharing is an odd sort of detached friendship and trust based solely on similar tastes in music or movies.

Uranus and Aquarius signify oddball, kooky individuals and trends. The Internet fosters quirky friendships. People in chat rooms don't know each other, yet they often become friends through a shared common interest that brought them to the chat room in the first place. The way language is altered for typing online instant messages is also quirky, new, and different.

Uranus and Aquarius are associated with independence. The cell phone's popularity skyrocketed while Uranus was in Aquarius. It was initially seen by older generations as nothing more than a cordless wall phone you could take out of the house. Teenagers, however, saw the cell phone as an independent way to relate, communicate, and foster connections. If you want to see the future, look at what teenagers are doing.

In fact, *The Economist* noted that cell phones bear a remarkable cultural resemblance to an earlier young generation's embrace of the automobile.[4] Mobile phones have become fashion statements that establish personal identity. The colors, styles, ring tones, and slipcovers of cellular phones all help young people to define themselves. They are symbols of teen independence—and you don't need a license to drive one. Teenagers are apt to comment, "Nice phone!"

Teenagers: Astrology Background

A universal fact about teenagers is that they all experience, around age fourteen, a sextile (60 degree angle) of transiting Uranus to natal Uranus. The sextile is an angle that facilitates the Uranus energy, making teenagers especially open and receptive to anything new and trendy. That is one reason why teenagers are worth observing if you want to see early cultural trends.

just as an earlier generation used to admire the latest cars. Ring tones have become like custom paint jobs were for teens of an earlier era. Cell phones, like cars, allow teens to get out of the house and explore the world on their own.

James Dean: Astrology Background

Aquarian James Dean had a powerful Fourth House Uranus which formed the middle part of a T-square. Saturn opposed a Jupiter-Pluto conjunction. This opposition was squared by Uranus, emptying intense rebellious energy into the Tenth House of public career.

Uranus, Fashion, and Half-Rebels

Uranus is the rebel wearing a black leather motorcycle jacket. American rebel icon (and Aquarius Sun) James Dean, star of *Rebel Without a Cause*, has a powerful Uranus in his horoscope.

While Neptune is fashion, Uranus is rebellious anti-fashion (punk chain metal belts or spike jewelry) which, in turn, can become its own fashion statement. Anti-fashion occurs when clothing becomes a symbol of rejection.

Uranus and Aquarius are also the "half-rebel"—quirky, kooky, oddball people and events. The public fascination with shock-rock singer Ozzy Osbourne's family life, as seen on TV, is reflected in the strong, rebellious Uranus in his horoscope. With Neptune in Aquarius until 2012, *The Osbournes* also reveals the public's continuing willingness to glamorize celebrities who display their quirks (see chapter 11 for more on this trend).

Uranus also represents rebellious or visionary music during any time period. For example, in late 1975, Uranus entered Scorpio, where it remained until 1981. Remember that Scorpio is ruled by dark and probing Pluto. In 1977, the Ramones in the U.S. and the Sex Pistols in England released albums which galvanized the trend toward punk rock music. Groups such as X and Black Flag soon followed.

Ozzy Osbourne: Astrology Background

Osbourne's Uranus opposes a Mars-Jupiter conjunction, this opposition forming the rim of a bowl pattern in his horoscope.

Uranus Profile: Nelson Mandela

Nelson Mandela was a South African leader who led the fight against apartheid. The apartheid system in South Africa was a form of segregation in which Africans were not allowed to vote, own land, or travel freely. After his political imprisonment, Mandela became his nation's first black president. When Uranus and Aquarius are combined, as they are in the horoscope of Nelson Mandela, there is a strong desire for freedom and equality. Mandela said that his urge toward freedom was deeply ingrained and seemed to have no external source. Liberation was part of his nature.[5]

Nelson Mandela has the Uranus and Aquarius quality of detachment. He is able to step back from any situation and not get emotionally involved. In many walks of life, this quality is a drawback. But for a leader who led a nation out of apartheid, detachment proved to be an asset. Nelson Mandela was a man seemingly without resentments or grudges. A lesser individual might have used his power to take revenge on the white South African power structure that had imprisoned him for twenty-seven years. Instead, Mandela showed how the power of ideals could sweep away the boundaries of color.

As a young man, Nelson Mandela became a leader of the African National Congress, which was dedicated to improving the living conditions of the black African majority in South Africa. In his twenties, he founded the first firm of black lawyers in South Africa. He defended poor and indigent South Africans, which allowed him to see firsthand the capricious racism of the apartheid legal system.[6] Mandela recounts in his autobiography the many indignities he had to face as a black lawyer in a white legal system. He met these insults with forbearance and a patient willingness to stand up for his rights as a human being. Mandela recalls his confrontation with a white police officer who tried to take him to the police station without arresting him. Expecting compliance, the police officer did not quite know how to respond to a black man who was willing to stand his ground—and cite the law.

Mandela was eventually tried for treason, with the government claiming that Mandela had been plotting a violent revolution. The treason trial collapsed, but he was again arrested and tried for sabotage. People who met him at this time in his life were amazed at how unfazed and optimistic he appeared in the face of adversity. Uranus can allow us to step back from a situation and feel free. This detachment can be a problem when intimacy is required, but when on political trial in the midst of apartheid, Uranus helps. Mandela's words at the end of his trial in 1964, when he faced a possible death penalty, are an eloquent testimony to the ideal of freedom:

> *I have cherished the ideal of a democratic and free society in which all persons live together in harmony and with equal opportunities. It is an ideal which I hope to live for and to achieve. But if needs be, it is an ideal for which I am prepared to die.*[7]

It was reported that at the end of this speech, the courtroom was so quiet that one could hear a pin drop.[8] Found guilty, Mandela was sentenced to life in prison. Uranus is the planet associated with the sky, and its power is such that even in a prison cell it can make the drab concrete ceiling into a blue firmament. Uranus can help us to rise above the sordidness of life and feel free. It helped Nelson Mandela to live and survive for twenty-seven years in a prison cell. His first years of imprisonment were spent in an all-black prison on Robben Island. His job there was to break rocks.

At one point, Mandela was guaranteed his freedom if he would renounce his membership in the African National Congress. He refused. His daughter read his reply at a rally held on his behalf: "I cherish my own freedom, but I care even more for your freedom. Your freedom and mine cannot be separated."[9]

He was finally released from prison after a worldwide "Free Mandela" campaign and changes in the white South African leadership. Mandela stepped out of prison on February 11, 1990. Some of his supporters suggested that, upon his release, he take a helicopter out of the prison. Mandela refused. He wanted the world to see him walk free.

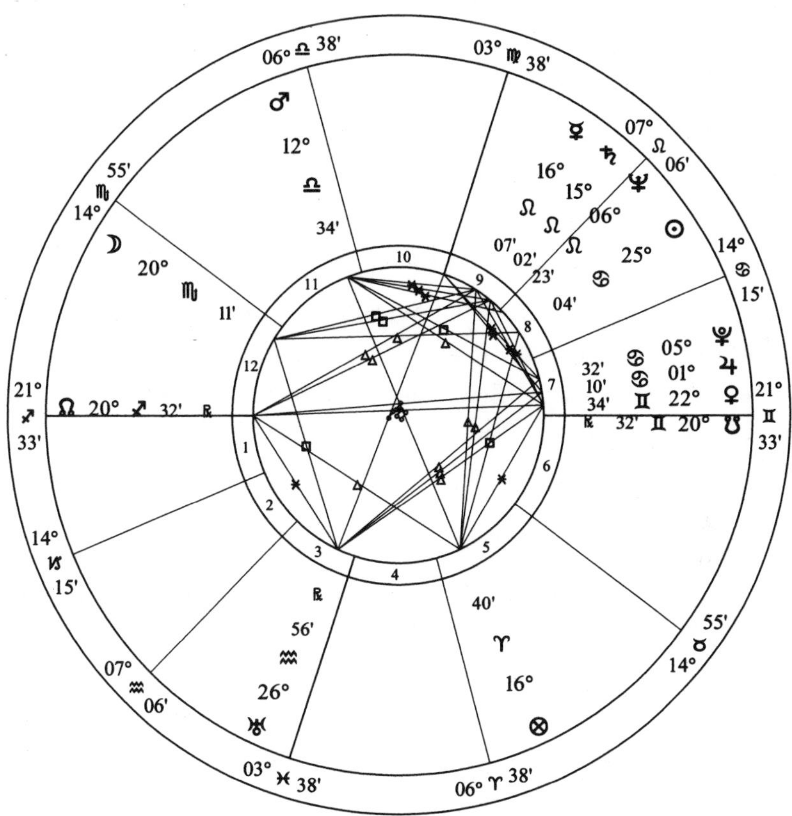

NELSON MANDELA
July 18, 1918 / 2:45 PM EET
Umtata, South Africa / Placidus houses

Nelson Mandela: Astrology Background

Nelson Mandela has a Uranus in Aquarius singleton in his chart, giving it a fundamental and seminal power in his life. He has the Uranian quality of being able to step back from any situation and not get emotionally involved. He also has the Sun, Jupiter, and Pluto all in nationalistic Cancer. On the day Mandela was released from prison, the Aquarian Sun was applying within four degrees of his Uranus, illuminating the planet of freedom.

Astro-Connections Activity

Future Planet Trends Worksheet

Outer Planet: ____________________________

Future sign (see Appendix D): __________________

Keyword combination (one planet keyword and one sign keyword):

____________________   ____________________

Write a paragraph describing **an imaginary** person who might fit the keyword combination (include clothing, home furnishings, hairstyle, headgear, likes, dislikes, and personality) OR draw a picture of an imaginary person who might fit the keyword combination.

Astro-Connections Activity

Creative Astrology Journals

Here are some creative journal topics to write about. You may also draw illustrations for these.

1. How would Uranus, Neptune, or Pluto furnish a restaurant and what would the menu look like?
2. Uranus has just moved into a new house or apartment. How would it be furnished? How about for Neptune or Pluto?
3. Imagine and describe a setting for a science-fiction movie or story that features Neptune, Uranus, or Pluto. That does not mean the story is set there, but rather that your description or illustration would have an astrological tone or mood. For example, a Neptunian setting might be misty and dreamlike.

Astro-Connections Activity

Fashion Trends

Observe fashion, paying careful attention to what young people are wearing, especially those who are old enough to choose their own clothes, hairstyles, and accessories. Notice the rebels and nonconformists since they are the first to tap into the emerging energies of Uranus, Neptune, and Pluto. We might not like the fashion, it might not be our own, but it does speak volumes about the future—a future we will soon inhabit. Observe youth fashions at malls, skateboard parks, movie theaters, and coffee shops.

Endnotes

1. Walter Isaacson, "In Search of the Real Bill Gates: Rebellion," *Time* online edition, 13 January 1997, http://www.time.com/time/gates/cover0.html (accessed 22 August 2006).
2. Doris Kearns Goodwin, *No Ordinary Time: Franklin and Eleanor Roosevelt: The Home Front in World War II* (New York: Simon and Schuster, 1994), 33, 35.
3. Lawrence Lessig, *The Future of Ideas: The Fate of the Commons in a Connected World* (New York: Random House, 2001), 19–23.
4. "Why Phones Are Replacing Cars," Economist.com, 29 April 2004, http://www.economist.com/displaystory.cfm?story_id=2628969 (accessed 22 August 2006).
5. Nelson Mandela, *Long Walk to Freedom: The Autobiography of Nelson Mandela* (New York: Little, Brown, and Company, 1995), 95.
6. Ibid., 149.
7. Ibid., 368.
8. *Mandela: Free at Last*, Globalvision, JCI Video, 79 minutes, 1990.
9. Ibid..

CHAPTER 10

Visions of Utopia: The Uranus-Neptune Conjunction

URANUS	NEPTUNE
Quirky	Idealized
Prophetic	Visionary
Rebellious	Fashion
Revolutionary	Drugs
Explosive	Merging
Inventive	Worship
Objective	Ephemeral
Technology	Glamorous
Utopian	Imagination
Quickening	Transcendence
Projecting	Yearning
Sudden awakening	Dissolving

When we look at major outer-planet patterns, it can be tempting to project disastrous events or sudden world change. However, astrologer Liz Greene points out that, at the time of a much-anticipated and feared planetary pattern in 1524, not much happened—except that an unknown monk named Martin Luther nailed some statements to a church door, and the Western world would never be the same again.[1]

Shifts in collective consciousness do not always shake the world like massive earthquakes. Sometimes, the change is more like developing a picture in a darkroom or putting on a new pair of glasses. This is especially true when we are looking at any pattern involving Neptune, a planet that does not like to be pinned down. When looking at influences of the outer planets, we need to pay attention to forces operating below the surface.[2]

Uranus and Neptune joined in 1993 when their orbital paths brought these two planets together for the first time in 172 years. Before 1993, the last time they had conjoined was in 1821. The Uranus-Neptune conjunction symbolizes utopian visions—the creation of a perfect world—arising out of global or national uncertainty and transition.

The conjunction of Uranus and Neptune brings new directions:

- It creates a powerful global yearning for a more perfect, utopian world.
- New economic foundations are laid.
- Massive social dislocations and disruptions take place.
- It creates a growing sense of personal powerlessness and willingness to believe in a "shadow world" of outside control.

Yearning for a More Perfect World

Individuals can more easily advance a utopian agenda in times when people are hungry for a new certainty and direction to rise out of the ashes of the old order. Utopia, the perfect world, can be a noble ideal or a march into some of history's greatest horrors. It can be a Union victory in the U.S. Civil War or it can be Hitler's catastrophic vision. The Uranus-Neptune conjunction leads to an intense global yearning for a more perfect world, but it does not tell us how to get there.

This planetary pattern coincides with historical periods of intense social and economic change. The Uranus-Neptune conjunction is revolutionary in the sense that old paradigms and hierarchies revolve or rotate.

In fact, one way to visualize the Uranus-Neptune conjunction is as a wheel that revolves when the conjunction becomes exact. Things that were on top of the wheel, at its highest point, will fall off and become lost if they are not fastened securely to the surface of the wheel. Something fastened securely to the surface will experience a change in position and may even end up on the bottom. Some things may even try to secure themselves so well that, like nails in a tire, they puncture or damage the wheel. That which was at the bottom will rotate to the top. It is a time of desperate confusion, jockeying for position, and newly forming hierarchies.

In the aftermath of the Uranus-Neptune conjunction, the 1990s were characterized by a frenzied reordering of culture. Although it proved to be ephemeral, forecasters spoke of a new paradigm. A visitor to the Silicon Valley near San Francisco during the late 1990s could marvel at the office buildings and displays of wealth that had sprung up seemingly overnight. Startup companies just two or three years old had office buildings displaying their names in bright neon. Many believed with all their hearts—and wallets—that this was indeed the new paradigm, the glorious future unfolding before our eyes. The stock market in the wake of the Uranus-Neptune conjunction also seemed to be a financial utopia that went in only one direction—up—at breathtaking speed.

The Berlin Wall was brought down just as the most recent Uranus-Neptune conjunction began to form (and as another conjunction, between Neptune and Saturn, became exact). Historian Joseph Rykwert has some observations about the aftermath of the fall of the Berlin Wall that are worth repeating here because they are descriptive of what we face in the wake of the Uranus-Neptune conjunction:

> *The city [of Berlin] was so shaken, its institutions so transformed, that it was unable to reshape itself for some time, while a mistrust of planning, perhaps all too understandable given the megalomania of the past, has meant that its government was not able to promulgate, much less embody, a plan for reconfiguring all of Berlin.*[3]

One can get a clear picture of the influence of the Uranus-Neptune conjunction by substituting "culture," society," or "the world" for "Berlin" in this quote.

New Economic Foundations

Uranus and Neptune met in the sign of Capricorn, the sign of the business world. New economic foundations are being built in the same way that the Industrial Revolution was transforming the world economy during the 1821 Uranus-Neptune conjunction. We will continue to see the elevation of the business ideal of the entrepreneur staking out a place in the world, but the new empires will be mental.[4]

We can already see this transformation taking place as old industries die, jobs are outsourced overseas, and a once-stable and reliable work world has given way to uncertainty and change. Many countries are even falling apart and disappearing.[5]

Other parts of culture also seem disconnected from old and reliable patterns. Individuals trying to make sense of the world will turn to those who seem to offer certainty and vision. It's a good time to be a snake oil salesperson. Businesses will also continue to try and present themselves as utopian—not only are they perfect for the world, but they are making themselves perfect for the consumer.

Large-Scale Social Change

The modern technology revolution will cause massive social dislocations, giving birth to a new utopian social philosophy. Uranus-Neptune in Capricorn symbolizes the creation of a new social system. The 1821 Uranus–Neptune conjunction ushered in the Victorian inequities of the Industrial Revolution, which in turn gave rise to Marxism. Karl Marx and Friedrich Engels—two of Communism's founders—were both born during the nineteenth century Uranus-Neptune conjunction. Communism's demise occurred around the time of the next Uranus-Neptune conjunction, completing a cycle.

Belief in a Shadow World

As economies and social systems change, individuals feel powerless in the face of large historical forces. It becomes much easier to blame one's fate on government and international conspiracies or a secret world that controls our lives. In fact, the markers for Uranus-Neptune include books, movies, and television shows portraying a supernatural or shadow world controlled by hidden forces.

The television show *The X-Files*, a mixture of government conspiracy and science fiction, debuted during the Uranus-Neptune conjunction. In addition to *The X-Files*, movies like *The Matrix* and *Men in Black* are the cinema of Uranus-Neptune.

Uranus-Neptune Profile: Clara Barton

The 1821 Uranus-Neptune conjunction was present at the birth of several notable political revolutionaries, visionaries, and humanitarians. Among these were Karl Marx and Frederich Engels, authors of *The Communist Manifesto*—which was written just after the planet Neptune was discovered, adding to its symbolism as the planet of utopian idealism;[6] Susan B. Anthony, a leader in the nineteenth century women's rights movement; hospital reformer Florence Nightingale; poet Walt Whitman; and Christian Science founder Mary Baker Eddy.

However, as the threat of terrorism makes the world an ever more dangerous place, it might help to focus on a person who embodies the humanitarian vision that can arise from war and calamity. The positive expression of the Uranus-Neptune conjunction is shown in the life of Clara Barton. Although this book deals with change, life's eternal verities are changeless. Love, compassion, and charity are not trends. Clara Barton's life shows how the planets connect us to these lasting truths of our existence.

Some who were born during the recent Uranus-Neptune conjunction will try to forcefully impose their utopian visions on the world, while others born under the same conjunction will reflect humanity's highest and noblest moral vision. The irony is that one will beget the other: several of the great Civil War generals who advanced the vision of national union on the battlefield, including William Tecumseh Sherman and Ulysses S. Grant, were born under the same Uranus-Neptune conjunction as Clara Barton—who had a vision of how to save those who were dying on those same battlefields.

Born in 1821 during the greatest intensity of the Uranus-Neptune conjunction, Clara Barton was the founder of the American Red Cross. She achieved a vision of service on the battlefields of the Civil War.

Army medical service at the time of the Civil War was a disgrace. When Clara Barton witnessed the terrible and untended injuries of Union soldiers straggling back into Washington after their defeat at the Battle of Bull Run, she formulated an idea of going to tend to these soldiers' wounds right on the battlefield.

Perhaps the most remarkable thing about Clara Barton was how she was able to sustain a vision of a more perfect world while in the midst of horrific battle scenes right out of Dante's *Inferno*. She would take a train filled with medical supplies, food, and drink to the front lines. When the train doors opened, she would be faced with the sight of thousands of wounded soldiers on the train platform and inside the station, waiting to be evacuated. The lack of battlefield medical care meant that many of the wounded had not been attended to and were screaming in agony. The ground was slippery with blood. Clara Barton would move among the men, offering crackers, bandages, sutures,

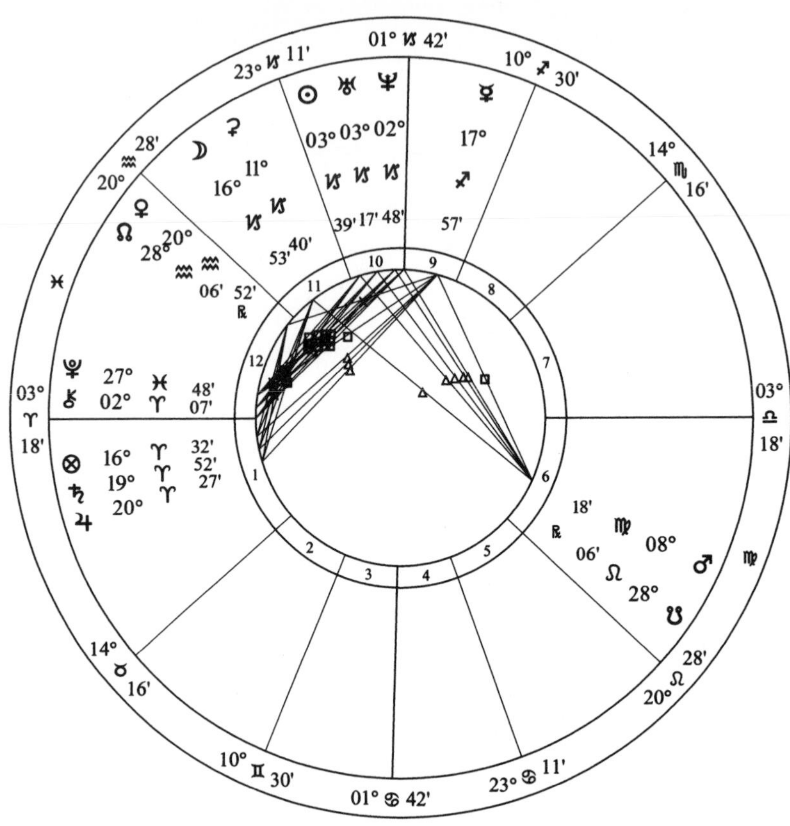

CLARA BARTON
December 25, 1821 / 11:52 AM LMT
Oxford, Bristol, MA / Placidus houses

water, whiskey, and loving words of encouragement. To survey a war scene of human torment and be able to maintain a vision of succor is Uranus-Neptune at its most refined and holds out hope that some born during the more recent 1993 conjunction of these two planets might rise to this compassionate level. In speaking of the experience of war, Clara Barton wrote, "Only the desire to soften some of its hardships and allay some of its miseries ever induced me . . . to dare its pestilence and unholy breath."[7]

She never married, although she loved and cared deeply for her own large extended family. She was sensitive to stimulants and intoxicants, as symbolized by a planetary pattern she shares with many others who have similar sensitivities. Clara Barton was also a vegetarian.

Barton was a woman in a man's battlefront and she had to fight to get there. She once remarked that men had tried to "carry the burdens of the world alone," but when men might have "the efficient help of woman he should be glad, and he will be."[8] She was an ardent feminist before the word was ever invented.

Clara Barton: Astrological Background

Clara Barton's horoscope has her Sun conjunct Uranus-Neptune at the highest point in her chart, the cusp of the Tenth House. She channeled, so to speak, the energy of the Uranus-Neptune conjunction through her own personal identity in a way that was evident for the world to see. Her extreme sensitivity to stimulants and intoxicants is a quality shared by many with close Sun-Neptune contacts in their charts, made even more pronounced by Uranus.

Astro-Connections Activity

Utopian Visions

Look for ways that a utopian vision is being expressed in culture. What are some ways you see people yearning for a more perfect world? How is this being expressed in your own community? Who are some individuals and groups who are expressing charity and finding new ways to do good in the world, particularly among young people? What are popular movies or songs that express a vision of a perfect world?

Endnotes

1. Greene, *The Outer Planets and Their Cycles*, 9.
2. Palden Jenkins, *Astrological Cycles in History*, http://cura.free.fr/xx/20palden.html (accessed 22 August 2006).
3. Joan Rykwert. *The Seduction of Place: The City in the Twenty-first Century* (New York: Pantheon Books, 2000), 340.
4. Juan Enriquez, *As the Future Catches You: How Genomics and Other Forces Are Changing Your Life, Work, Health, and Wealth* (New York: Crown Business, 2001), 59.
5. Ibid., 45.
6. In a scathingly satiric work titled *The Condition of the Working Class in England* (New York: Oxford University Press, 1999), Friedrich Engels observed the inequities of working-class life in Victorian England in 1845.
7. Stephen B. Oates, *A Woman of Valor: Clara Barton and the Civil War* (New York: The Free Press, 1994), 382.
8. Ibid., 379.

CHAPTER 11

Uranus and Neptune Star in *Trading Signs*

The 1960s and 1970s were notable for their inner-directedness. Finding one's personal identity was what mattered most. This was due in part to the self-absorption of the Pluto in Leo generation. However, it was also because of the sign placements of Uranus, Neptune, and Pluto, all of which are now lined up in a different, more outer-directed pattern. Large-scale astrological events raise world tensions rather than consciousness.

Uranus, Neptune, and Pluto have always affected global and national events, but the world today is much more connected. There is an astrological butterfly effect. When Neptune gently flutters its wings in some remote part of the globe, we feel hurricane-strength wind gusts half a world away.

Above the Horizon: Astrology Background

One of the most interesting developments in charting the astrology of Uranus, Neptune, and Pluto is that all three are traveling through signs considered to be indicative of large-scale and global affairs. This contrasts sharply with earlier decades. In the 1960s, for example, both Uranus and Pluto were "below the horizon" as their natural orbits took them through Virgo (see chapter 14 for more on the Uranus-Pluto conjunction). Presently, Uranus, Neptune, and Pluto are all in signs that are considered to be above the horizon, occupying a part of the zodiac that is focused on the outer, rather than the inner, world.

NEPTUNE (Ruler of Pisces)	AQUARIUS (Ruled by Uranus)
Idealized	Ideas
Visionary	Society
Fashion	Internet
Drugs	Egalitarian
Merging	Detachment
Worship	Revolution
Ephemeral	Technology
Glamorous	Globalization
Imagination	Public domain
Transcendence	Airwaves
Yearning	Groups

URANUS (Ruler of Aquarius)	PISCES (Ruled by Neptune)
Quirky	Escape
Prophetic	Beauty
Rebellious	Artistic
Revolutionary	Unreality
Explosive	Creativity
Inventive	Ambiguity
Objective	Uniformity
Technology	Spirituality
Utopian	Compassion
Quickening	Loneliness
Projecting	Sensitivity

Just like popular television shows in which people trade houses in order to better appreciate what they have, Uranus and Neptune have traded signs.

Imagine a television show called *Trading Signs*. In this show, Neptune and Uranus trade the signs they each rule and do some redecorating. Neptune rules Pisces and Uranus rules Aquarius. If they trade signs, Neptune goes to live in Aquarius for a little while and Uranus moves into Pisces.

There's not enough feeling and sensitivity in Aquarius, so Neptune injects a bit of touchy-feely redecorating by putting in softer colors and replacing the cold-looking blue color Uranus seems to have favored. Neptune puts in cushiony sofas and furniture that you can sink into. Tiffany lamps and little glass unicorns are part of the new Neptune decor.

Uranus, on the other hand, takes one look at the Pisces interior and starts to turn it into a "smart home." The refrigerator is programmed to beep when the milk is low. The nice Impressionist art prints on the walls are replaced with abstract sculptures made out of car parts and coat hangers. The soft furniture is replaced with molded black plastic chairs and glass tables. Of course, the two planets are okay with all this because they agreed to be on the show in the first place and they can always change it back later.

Uranus entered the sign of Pisces in 2003, where it will remain until 2011. Neptune entered Aquarius in 1998 and will be there until 2012. Since Uranus rules Aquarius and Neptune rules Pisces, the two planets have traded signs, a phenomenon astrologers call "mutual reception." This phenomenon intensifies the merging energies of these two planets that began with the Uranus-Neptune conjunction discussed in chapter 10.

This chapter will help you to spot some mutual reception trends that are happening now or are just about to happen:

- The merging of technology, language, celebrity, and culture will result in new definitions of ourselves and our world.
- Computerized art will be displayed in major museums alongside Picasso and Monet.
- Soon-to-be-discovered celebrities and performers who can project images of glamorous rebellion will capture the public imagination.
- Celebrity worship will reach new extremes. Kooky, odd-ball celebrities will continue to entertain us with real-life performances.
- Some facets of the Internet will be recognized as acting like an addictive drug, and people will start forming self-help groups.
- We will feel threatened by secret enemies and underground societies.
- Fashions will continue to be ever more egalitarian.

Interconnectedness

We are living in a world that is connected as never before. Neptune dissolves boundaries while Aquarius opens up the airwaves. As the connections continue to form new, ever more tangled webs, the complexity of our world will grow exponentially.

At the same time, the world has shrunk to the size of a voice connection. Customer service call centers have been set up in foreign countries like India. However, the call monitors ("This call may be monitored for quality assurance purposes") are not sitting in the same room with the customer service representative. They are likely to be in a place like Long Island, New York, listening to the Indian customer service operator talk to someone in San Francisco.[1]

The Internet fosters new social networks. Boundaries and distances that used to inhibit social exchanges are now easily crossed through the Internet. From a home in the U.S., one can communicate effortlessly via e-mail or instant messages with friends overseas. A stop at a cyber café can put travelers in instant touch with friends and family back home. Neptune is diffusion in Aquarius, the borderless air.

The rapid evolution of cell phones demonstrates the power of the mutual reception of Uranus and Neptune. Because of their size and portability, cellular phones can serve a number of uses. Some banks may soon allow cell phones to be used for the same functions as a bank debit card when all we want to purchase is a candy bar or a magazine. Many cell phones now are wirelessly connected to the Internet. If I am browsing in a store and see a product I like, with my cell phone I can instantly go online and do a little comparison shopping to see if I can get the same item for a better price somewhere else, and then place my order while I'm in the competitor's store.[2]

Aquarius represents control of air—including the airwaves of radio, television, cell phones, and wireless technology.[3] If Neptune in Aquarius signifies the spread of wireless technology, the co-rulership of Aquarius by Saturn (see chapter 3) indicates its control—by government, individuals, or corporations. Battles to control the airwaves will grow in intensity.

Neptune also breaks down borders in some unusual ways. A non-technological way in which the mutual reception of Uranus and Neptune has dissolved boundaries and fostered connections is animal-human communications. Beginning with Monty Roberts's book *The Man Who Listens to Horses,* published just before Neptune entered Aquarius in 1998, there has been a great interest in communications between animals and people. When Uranus entered Pisces, interest in this area intensified and is certain to grow over the next few years.

Computer Art

Uranus, an inventive planet, "quickens" whatever sign it is passing through, while Neptune softens and lends an artistic eye to the sign through which it is traveling. As Uranus moves through Pisces and Neptune through Aquarius, we will see a quickening of artistic applications in computer technology. Movies are already in the midst of a digital revolution that will only increase as Uranus projects itself onto the moving Piscean screen (see chapter 12).

Computerized art will be displayed in museums, much like the video art of Bill Viola, whose video installation *The Passions* has been displayed at major museums. Nam June Paik's *Video Flag Z* consisted of seventy video monitors and four laser disc players—until it had to be put in museum storage when parts could not be found to replace its aging 1980s technology.[4] We can expect to see computers used for similar major art installations. Computer art will be very different from what can be created on one monitor using sophisticated drawing and animation software. Instead, computer art will use the medium of computer software, hardware, and multiple monitors to create an amazing grid or sculpture that reflects back on modern technology itself and our place in a digital world. Computer art may connect with various museums for a simultaneous global art installation. It will make a statement about the medium it uses.

Celebrity Worship

Neptune is the planet of fantasy, dreams, and illusions. It rules the modern frenzy of celebrity worship. In a book called *Within the Context of No Context,* George W. S. Trow traced the modern celebrity culture from the covers of *Life* to the pages of *People*. Celebrities have come down from the Mt. Olympus heights of *Life* magazine and into our family rooms and bedrooms. Trow writes of two grids. One is composed of the entire population of the United States and the other is a grid of celebrities. The merging of the two grids is now a commonplace way to manipulate magazine sales and TV viewership. When we can feel one with celebrities, we have achieved a measure of worth.[5] This is intensified when Uranus and Neptune trade signs.

During Neptune's passage through quirky, airy Aquarius—and the mutual reception with Uranus in Pisces—we have seen the growing popularity of oddball celebrities. Rock star Ozzy Osbourne, the Prince of Darkness, prepared breakfast for his family in Beverly Hills on the reality TV show *The Osbournes.* On another reality TV show, *Newlyweds: Nick & Jessica,* newlywed (at the time) pop superstar Jessica Simpson, the world's smartest airhead, learned to overcome her fear of dolphins and control a vacuum cleaner. Both shows were big hits and catapulted Ozzy Osbourne and Jessica Simpson to a different kind of stardom, one in which their foibles and eccentricities became endearing. These Neptune in Aquarius/Uranus in Pisces television shows merge the grid of stardom with the grid of ourselves.

Glamorous Rebels

Another trading-signs trend is the glamorous, independent rebel. For example, Carrie Bradshaw, the character played by actress Sarah Jessica Parker on *Sex and the City,* wore hip, cutting-edge fashions. She was determinedly single, rebelling against marriage and the fairy tale of the Shining Prince until the very last episode.

More glamorous rebels will hit the spotlight until Neptune passes into its own watery sign of religious Pisces, at which time we will be awash in celebrity worship.

One of the first of the glamorous celebrity rebels was Buffalo Bill Cody, star of his own Wild West Show. He was born in 1846, during Neptune's last transit through Aquarius.

Buffalo Bill Cody's Wild West shows staged the frontier for audiences in the late nineteenth century. His shows were wildly successful and brought him fame in Europe as well as America. Much like the modern celebrities who become famous for being themselves, Cody was famous for bringing his own life as a frontier scout to the stage and giving audiences a taste of the "Wild West"—complete with cowboy and Indian battles that would be considered

Buffalo Bill Cody: Astrology Background

Cody's horoscope reveals four planets, including the Sun, in Neptune-ruled Pisces. All of the planets in his horoscope are tightly grouped within 80 degrees. Astrologers call this a bundle pattern and it reveals a tremendous amount of self-contained personal energy.

racist by today's standards. He helped to create, nurture, and fuel a cult of celebrity worship that continues to this day. Buffalo Bill Cody and his contemporaries showed mass audiences that it was possible for anyone—even a Wild West frontier scout—to achieve fame and fortune in America.[6]

Neptune in Aquarius has dissolved the line between "us" and "them." We are celebrities and celebrities are us. A teenage star can grow up and enter rehab. just like a regular person. Unknown individuals can become bachelor, bachelorette, and survivor celebrities, or American idols just like real celebrities. In fact, *American Idol* loser William Hung was so charmingly bad he became famous and got a huge record deal.[7]

Advertising

Neptune is marketing and Aquarius is an air sign. Neptune in Aquarius has given us marketing—which is in the air, everywhere.

The boundaries have been eroded to the point where there is no longer a line dividing us from technology. With Neptune in Aquarius, marketing has saturated our environment. It's even on the floors in supermarkets, so when you look down at your grocery list, you'll be sure to see an ad.

Business has more and more taken on the qualities of Neptune because so much of modern business is based not on selling a product, but on selling an idea or a concept. *Fish! A Remarkable Way to Boost Morale and Improve Results* was a popular motivational book published in 2000. The ideas contained in the book are based on teamwork at Seattle's Pike Place fish market. It is very Neptunian and Piscean, using the idea of throwing and catching slippery fish to build teamwork.

Online Addiction

The online world has become addictive. Many individuals, when deprived of their online fix, report feelings of withdrawal, disconnectedness, and loss.[8] When they want answers to life's vexing problems, many people turn not to friends, spouses, spiritual guides, or trusted elders, but rather to Google, which has become for many individuals the twenty-first century's most trusted source of knowledge and wisdom. From using it at the workplace to checking a new music video to planning a weekend getaway, the Internet has become indispensable to millions.

Addictive Neptune

Neptune and Pisces are often associated with drugs and alcohol. The sign element—earth, air, fire, or water—through which Neptune is traveling relates to the waxing and waning popularity of particular drugs. The unfortunate caveat must be added that drugs and alcohol in general are never out of fashion.

Neptune's passage through watery Scorpio in the late eighteenth and early part of the nineteenth centuries coincided with England's addictive and popular consumption of laudanum, a liquid opium extract. Under its influence, Romantic poet Samuel Taylor Coleridge envisioned "an incense-bearing tree/...A savage place! as holy and enchanted/As e'er beneath a waning moon was haunted..."[10] Neptune's transit through Scorpio a century and a half later, in the 1960s, saw the popular use of another liquid drug, LSD.

The 1920s, when Neptune was in fun and fiery Leo, are often associated with hard liquor consumption. Ernest

continued...

Neptune and Pisces are the astrological symbols of drugs and intoxication. During the transit of Neptune in Aquarius, the Internet delivered a new drug: instant pornography. Following a well-worn addictive path, Internet pornography addiction appears to mimic the brain responses of crack cocaine.[9]

Secret Enemies and Underground Societies

The sign-trading of Neptune and Uranus has helped create secret enemies, underground movements, and occult societies. These are related especially to Pisces, but we also find their expression through Neptune in Aquarius.

Occult societies can appear on the bestseller list. The best-selling novel *The Da Vinci Code* was first released in March 2003—just as Uranus entered Pisces. *The Da Vinci Code* spawned its own cottage industry, with follow-up books such as *Secrets of the Code.* More than most bestsellers, it burrowed its way deep into popular culture. Eighteen months after it was published, *The Da Vinci Code* was number one on the *New York Times* fiction bestseller list.

The Da Vinci Code opens with a murdered Louvre Museum curator who leaves behind clues leading to a chase through history, art, religion, and myth. The murdered curator was also a high-ranking member of a secret church society that had been protecting secrets about the life of Christ for two thousand years. The novel's symbologist hero and cryptographer heroine try to solve the murder mystery, and in the process they delve into some of history's greatest unsolved mysteries, including the art of Leonardo da Vinci, the Holy Grail, and the life of Christ. What seems to have attracted readers are the shadowy, esoteric mysteries and occult societies.

Sometimes, secret enemies are just a keystroke away. Hackers are individuals who gain unauthorized access to computer systems by breaking software codes to steal and corrupt data. They are a real-life secret society that continues to plot in underground chat rooms, looking for vulnerabilities in computer operating systems and web browsers.

E-mail has become fogged and clogged with secret enemies: phishing, viruses, and spyware. Phishing, a Piscean word derived from the word "fishing," is the sending of fake company e-mails requesting credit card numbers, passwords, or other personal information.[11]

With Uranus in the constellation of conspiratorial Pisces, spyware operates underground and can allow someone to control a personal computer, see the contents of a hard drive, even monitor keystrokes. Some computer users are finding that their computers have become so dysfunctional that the entire hard drive needs to be erased for a fresh start.

Hemingway's classic "Lost Generation" novel, *The Sun Also Rises*—set in France and Spain in the 1920s—contains so much heavy drinking that one can almost smell the whiskey and see wine stains on the pages. However, it was also the time of a Jupiter-Saturn conjunction (these set the tone every twenty years and are discussed in more detail in chapter 15) in moralistic Virgo. So we had Prohibition *and* heavy drinking.

While Neptune was in the earth sign Capricorn, between 1984 and 1998, the popularity of coca-based cocaine soared and medical marijuana laws were passed.

With Neptune in the air sign of Aquarius between 1998 and 2012, a new air addiction has surfaced—Internet pornography. This may become the twenty-first century's secret and anonymous addictive disease, much as alcoholism was the twentieth century's.

Egalitarian Fashions

Egalitarian fashions are clothes and accessories that are designed for both men and women. Egalitarian fashions are popular—look at boyish hair lengths for women and jewelry for men. The television show *Queer Eye for the Straight Guy* captures this spirit of the equalizing nature of apparel.

A Neptune in Aquarius prediction: look for Internet fashions—no, not clothes bought over the Internet, but fashions with wireless Internet devices embedded in the actual clothing.

Technology Worship

The last time Neptune was in an air sign was in the 1950s, when it was in Libra, the beginning of the modern glamorization of television.

Today, technology and the Internet are glamorized, even worshipped. Walk into any electronics store and gaze at the computer displays. The computers are sleek black and silver embodiments of technological power. Their screens display colorful interactive graphics. Computers rival clothing as the most enticing retail displays anywhere. Since Neptune entered Aquarius (the sign of modern technology, and the connected world) in early 1998, computers and the Internet have found their way into virtually every workplace, library, and home in the United States.

Uranus in Pisces, a water sign, will give us more liquid technologies. Gas is used in plasma TV. Some new Macintosh computers use liquid cooling systems. Car companies are starting to develop hydrogen fuel cells as an alternative fuel for automobiles. Hydrogen fuel cells are devices that can power a car with electrons generated from hydrogen, producing a water vapor exhaust instead of the usual smog pollutants. It's another Uranus in Pisces development, likely to grow through 2011.

Neptune in Aquarius Profile: American Utopian Colonies

> *If a man does not keep pace with his companions, perhaps it is because he hears a different drummer. Let him step to the music which he hears, however measured or far away.*
>
> —from *Walden,* by Henry David Thoreau

Neptune and Uranus also traded signs between 1835 and 1842, with Neptune continuing in Aquarius until 1848 (both planets will end the current mutual reception at about the same time, Uranus in 2011 and Neptune in 2012). During the nineteenth century mutual reception, a number of individuals were inspired to try to live out utopian ideals in different colonies, centered primarily in the northeastern United States. A look at this period of American history offers vivid proof of how the outer planets affect culture and society, which also has implications for our own culture over the next decade as individuals seek to build communities (including online virtual communities) that reflect their spiritual, moral, and educational ideals.

In 1841, Ralph Waldo Emerson published a series of essays. The most famous and influential of these essays was "Self-Reliance," in which Emerson wrote:

> *Whoso would be a man must be a nonconformist. He who would gather immortal palms must not be hindered by the name of goodness, but must explore if it be goodness. Nothing is at last sacred but the integrity of your own mind. I hope in these days we have heard the last of conformity and consistency.*[12]

Emerson's ideals influenced the subsequent establishment of nonconformist utopian communities, which reached their heights in the 1840s.

The experimental community Brook Farm was established when Neptune was in Aquarius and Uranus was in Pisces—just as they are today. Brook Farm existed from 1841 until 1847. Emerson was a supporter, but he did not join the actual community. About one hundred residents of Brook Farm in Massachusetts created an environment of physical labor, individual self-culture, strong schooling, and an active social life. They tried to put into practice Emerson's theories. Writer Nathaniel Hawthorne briefly resided at Brook Farm and later wrote *Blithedale Romance,* a novel that gently satirizes an experiment in communal living.

Another utopian community, Fruitlands, was established by Amos Bronson Alcott (the father of *Little Women* author Louisa May Alcott) in 1843. Alcott was very influenced by Emerson and had made a point of looking at—and rejecting—other utopian communities that were springing up in and around New England.[13] Fruitlands emphasized manual labor, a vegetarian diet, religious harmony, and education. Its residents included a male nudist, a former Brook Farmian who was on a special diet of apples and crackers, and one woman.

Fruitlands did not last long, but after it disbanded Alcott helped in the construction of a one-man utopia: Henry David Thoreau's cabin at Walden Pond. In it, Thoreau began his experiment in applied Transcendental living in 1845.

The most successful of the utopian communities established during this period was Oneida in New York. Founded by John Noyes, the Oneida group practiced "Bible Communism," applying biblical precepts to communal living. The residents of Oneida contributed a number of different crafts, including broom manufacturing, shoe manufacturing, flour processing, and lumber milling. They held communal property, fixed meals together in an egalitarian kitchen, and shared the rearing and education of children. Oneida was founded near the end of Neptune in Aquarius and lasted until 1881. The most controversial element of the community was a free-love doctrine called complex marriage, a form of polygamy.

Considering that these utopian colonies were established in reaction to the Industrial Revolution, one wonders what reactions might spring from the twenty-first-century information revolution and the current transits of Neptune through Aquarius and Uranus in Pisces.

Astro-Connections Activity

Trends Squares

Use the following model to help spot trends. In the circle in the middle of the two squares, write down a keyword for Uranus, Neptune, or Pluto, or a keyword combination. In the squares, write down two new trends, social developments, news stories, inventions, or gadgets that match the word or words in the circle. I've done a sample for you, using the keywords "Artistic Technology" for Uranus (technology) in Pisces (artistic). Artistic expressions can include music and design. Uranus will be in Pisces until 2011.

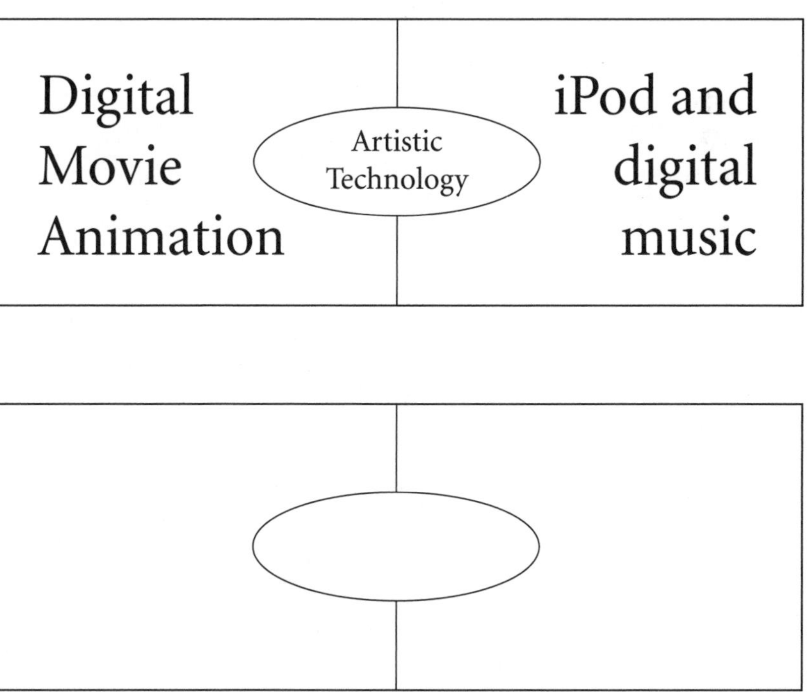

Astro-Connections Activity

Three-Bubble Chart

The following chart is designed to chart connections between keywords. In one box, write a keyword for Uranus, Neptune, or Pluto, and in the other box write a keyword for the sign it's in. Then, in the circles, write the names of people, places, or things in culture that connect the two keywords. I've completed a sample for Neptune in Aquarius so you can see how it's done.

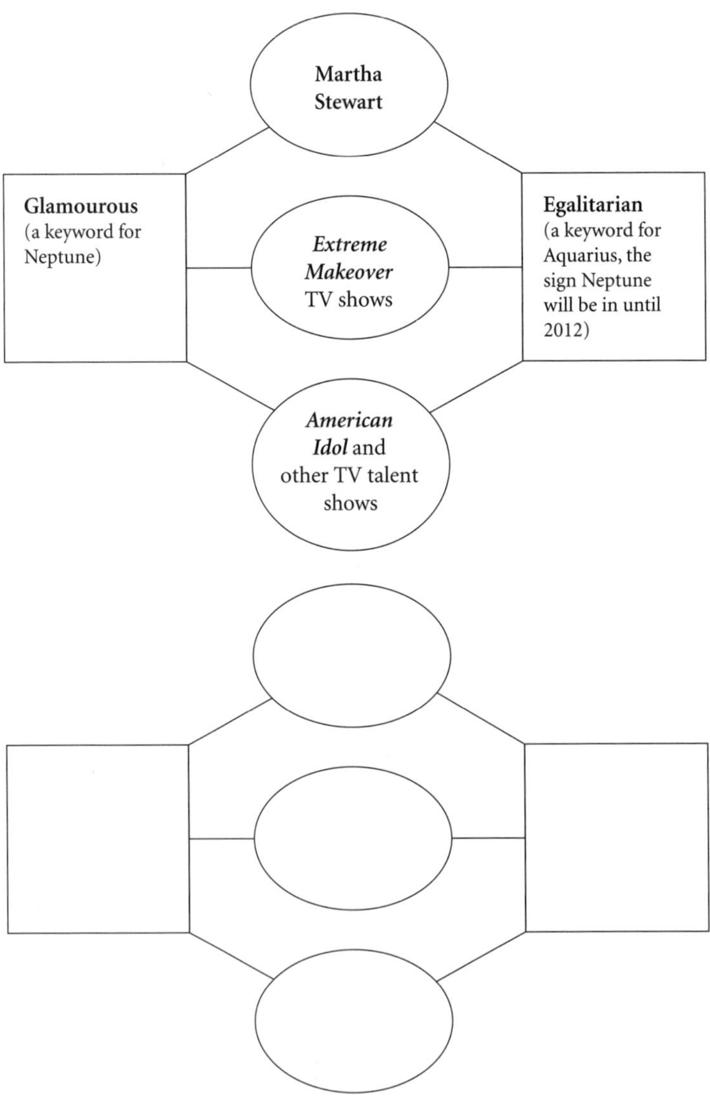

ENDNOTES

1. Ken Belson, "Your Call (and Rants on Hold) Will Be Monitored," *The New York Times*, 11 January 2005, late ed.: A1.

2. "Master of the Youniverse," Trendwatching.com, http://www.trendwatching.com/trends/MASTERoftheYOUNIVERSE.htm (accessed 23 August 2006).

3. Dale O'Brien, "Control of Thought and Emotion with Aquarian Airwaves," *International Society for Astrological Research Member Electronic Newsletter*, Volume 310, 14 November 2004.

4. Alex Pham, "Art That Goes on the Blink," *The Los Angeles Times*, 4 October 2004: A1.

5. George W. S. Trow, *Within the Context of No Context* (New York: Atlantic Monthly Press, 1980), 48.

6. Leo Braudy, *The Frenzy of Renown: Fame and Its History* (New York: Vintage Books, 1997), 509–510.

7. "William Hung Lands Record Deal," CBSNews.com, 6 April 2004, http://www.cbsnews.com/stories/2004/04/05/earlyshow/leisure/music/main610305.shtml (accessed 22 August 2006).

8. "Yahoo! and OMD Reveal Study Depicting Life Without The Internet," Yahoo! Media Relations Press Release, 22 September 2004, http://docs.yahoo.com/docs/pr/release1183.html (accessed 22 August 2006).

9. "Senate Hears Testimony on Porn Addiction," USA Today.com, 18 November 2004, http://www.usatoday.com/news/washington/2004-11-18-senate-porn_x.htm (accessed 22 August 2006).

10. Samuel Taylor Coleridge, "Kubla Khan," *The Norton Anthology of English Literature: Fifth Edition*, ed. M. H. Abrams (New York: W. W. Norton & Company, 1986), 354.

11. Tom Spring, in "Spam Slayer: Do You Speak Spam?" (PCWorld.com, 17 November 2003, http://www.pcworld.com/article/id,113431-page,1/article.html , accessed 22 August 2006), notes that the origin of the word "phishing" is not related to the rock group Phish. It is common among the computer-hacker subculture to substitute "ph" for "f," as in the slang word "phreak."

12. Ralph Waldo Emerson, "Self-Reliance," *Ralph Waldo Emerson: Essays and Lectures* (New York: Library of America, 1983), 261.

13. Geraldine Brooks, "Orpheus at the Plow," *The New Yorker*, 10 January 2005: 58–65.

CHAPTER 12

Future Trends with Uranus and Neptune

In this chapter, you will learn how the mutual reception of Uranus and Neptune will affect three specific trends:

- Biogenetics and the science of the human genome will revolutionize our world and our personal identities.
- Robots will become commonplace.
- Movies and home entertainment will transport us into a new realm of digital imagination.

Biogenetics and the Human Genome[1]

The emerging discoveries of genomics—the study of the complete set of human genes—are about to shake our personal identities, much as Copernicus jolted astronomy and Freud shook the psyche.

One month after Uranus entered Pisces in 2003, the Human Genome Project was completed[2], marking another milestone on an astrological continuum that can be traced all the way back to the Uranus–Neptune conjunction of 1821. From the gardens of the monk-geneticist Gregor Mendel to the computer models of the human genome, planetary threads are being woven into an astro-genetic tapestry that has yet to be finished.

The human genome is the complete set of about thirty thousand human genes. These genes are on winding DNA molecules packed into our twenty-three pairs of chromosomes and located in each cell of the human body. Genes are coded messages attached like stairsteps or ladder rungs to the double spiral chains of DNA molecules. The various combinations of the code—simple rearrangements of four chemical structures—and the order in which the rungs are arranged spell out the information stored in the genes. With the completion of the Human Genome Project, scientists have transcribed the code of each gene, although they do not yet know what each gene does.

Genomics is already beginning to change our perceptions of who we are and the choices we make. Our concept of personal identity has been radically and fundamentally altered at various times throughout history, and this is starting to happen again now because of biogenetic discoveries.

One of the underlying symbols of the Uranus–Neptune conjunction of 1993—reinforced through the present mutual reception of Uranus and Neptune (see chapter 11)—is the mapping of the human genome and its implications for the future. While Uranus was in Aquarius, the world witnessed a revolution in personal technology. Now that Uranus has entered Pisces, we are seeing a similar revolution in biogenetics.

Genomics marks the intersection of the computer, robotics, and biogenetics. Computers and robotics are essential for handling and processing vast stores of information on genetic material: there are more than three billion pieces of data in the double-helix spirals of the human genome. Just as computers shifted from relative isolation into mass use, from mainframe to Macintosh/PC to Windows to the Internet, biogenetics will begin to broaden its reach. Right now it is in the lab, beginning to seep out into the culture—but it has not hit us yet. Here are some ways we will be affected by emerging genomic discoveries:

- Pharmaceuticals will be marketed as niche products targeted to individual genotypes.
- Gene chips will lead to personalized medicine, and we may take daily pills that are targeted to our specific genetic conditions.[3]
- As scientists uncover more connections between our genes and environmental triggers, vitamins and herbs will continue to grow in popularity. These natural dietary supplements will be seen as ways to increase genomic vitality.
- Bio-informatics is a new field that uses computer models to predict results of biological lab experiments.[4] It is a new Uranus in Pisces career.

- Another Uranus in Pisces profession, bio-data processing, will be needed in order to store all the information that scientists are finding in our genomes and the genomes of other species.

Cloning

In 2008, when Pluto enters Capricorn—a sign associated with aging—cloning developments will move to the forefront of our lives. Cloning is genetic duplication, creating an identical genetic twin. Many forms of cloning are already taking place; human cloning is but an extreme version.

Dolly, the cloned sheep, aged rapidly and died prematurely because the genes from which she was cloned were from an older sheep. Other cloning experiments have actually resulted in just the opposite: *increased* longevity. In our youth-obsessed culture, people will soon look to cloning as a new fountain of youth. This does not mean that people will clone themselves. Rather, cloned body parts will have cosmetic applications.

The cloning of embryonic stem cells for transplantation in the treatment of disease has generated intense political debate in the United States, but several other countries have passed legislation allowing this form of cloning. Aging is one area of molecular biology being studied with increasing intensity.

A Brave New World?

The conjunction of Uranus and Neptune in 1993 (see chapter 10) was followed ten years later by their entering into mutual reception. The shared energies of Uranus and Neptune have ushered in a time of extraordinary—and perilous—possibilities.

Aldous Huxley wrote of some of the perils of biogenetics in his cautionary novel *Brave New World*. In this dystopian tale, Huxley portrays a dehumanized future society of bio-engineered genetic uniformity and mass cloned reproduction. Children are educated with a series of Pavlovian instructional techniques designed to prepare them for planned social roles. Society is run as a big business.

This may be the potential dark side of Uranus in Pisces, intensified through the mutual reception of Neptune in Aquarius and soon to be accompanied by Pluto in Capricorn. In a startling twenty-first century parallel to Huxley's vision, scientists are now hailing experimental results showing that lab monkeys who were given brain injections to suppress a certain gene were transformed from lazy simians into energetic, task-oriented primates.[5]

There is also an alternative, brighter vision of the biogenetic future. Pisces has to do with the collective unconscious, the liquid archetypal depths where we are all connected and the surface differences between us have washed away. The study of the human genome has revealed the startling degree to which our genes are connected. Perhaps the human genome, which binds us all in so many ways, is a manifestation of the collective unconscious.

Every person on earth shares 99.9 percent of the same genome. The other 0.1 percent is what makes us individuals. Our genetic connections far outweigh our differences. The exploration of the human genome offers the possibility of a gentler, kinder genomic future, during which we might eventually come to understand our essential unity.

Uranus Never Sleeps: The Astrology of Robots

Robots are set to capture the public imagination, much like the Internet in the 1990s or personal computers in the early 1980s. Over the next several years, we will see rapid development in Piscean areas such as medicine and health care—with robotics leading the way.

Science-fiction books and movies have long forecast the widespread use of human-like robots. Science-fiction writer Isaac Asimov's 1942 short story "Runaround," which featured a robotic world, was later published as part of a collection of stories in *I, Robot*. This book later became the basis for the 2004 movie of the same name, starring Will Smith. It showed robots as commonplace, all-purpose drudges—schlepping shopping bags and hailing taxis—until they staged a peasants' revolt.

The popular media have also depicted colorful androids in movies like *Blade Runner* and robots with attitudes, such as the irascible C-3PO from *Star Wars*. Cyberpunk fiction writer William Gibson, in novels such as *Mona Lisa Overdrive,* portrays a world in which robots mingle uneasily with the down-and-out in a futuristic urban landscape.

The robots of science fiction are about to become a reality. We will begin to witness the glamorization and spread of robotics. The use of robots is set to take off, with robot vacuum cleaners and lawn mowers leading the vanguard of a revolution in home technology.[6]

Uranus, the modern planetary ruler of airy Aquarius, is invention and technological wizardry. Neptune, the modern ruler of liquid Pisces, has to do with things that seep into all areas of life. Neptune also rules the popular imagination, glamour, and things we glamorize through mass media. The mutual exchange of these two planets has helped to set the stage for the robot revolution and will make robots—automatic devices that perform functions normally carried out by humans—a huge social and cultural trend. In the years ahead, we will find that the world warms to cool, metallic robots in surprising ways.

A look into the past can help us to see the future. Uranus takes eighty-four years to go through all twelve signs of the zodiac. The last time Uranus was in Pisces, its current sign, was in the 1920s. By looking back at events in part of that decade, we can begin to project some possibilities for the present and near future. In the 1920s, the nation witnessed a technological revolution that was very similar to what we are seeing now. In the 1920s, devices such as pop-up toasters, hair dryers, and bread slicers helped make for more efficient households. In addition, the shortwave radio was introduced and, not coincidentally, the first robot was produced.

Over the last decade, technology has exploded. Both Uranus in Pisces and Neptune in Aquarius are characterized by technology in the public domain rather than in the hands of a privileged few. We have seen the growth of the Internet, lightning-fast personal computer processors, digital cameras, cellular phone technology—and, soon, robots. This modern technology is distinguished by its wide accessibility and popular use. Only a few went to the moon. Millions log on to the Internet. It will be the same with robots. They will be everywhere.

Out of the Lab and Into the Battlefield

Large-scale technological advances are frequently developed by the military and research laboratories, often working in tandem. The early ENIAC computer, for example, was originally built to chart munitions trajectories. The military is in the process of developing robots for a number of battlefield tasks, such as minesweeping.[7] Scientific labs use robots as drones to perform onerous physical tasks like swabbing slides. Many of these military and scientific uses will begin to have applications in our homes. What makes the coming robot revolution so different from the robots used on factory assembly lines is that the new revolution will produce robots that are adaptable to different environments. Pisces, the sign in which the technology planet Uranus currently resides, is known for being adaptable and flexible. Small robots can be programmed to silently vacuum the carpet twice a week, even when the furniture has been rearranged.

The robot revolution began in earnest when a robot named Spirit landed on Mars—and, unlike an earlier attempt, this time it worked. So did the next robot, Opportunity, which landed three weeks later. In an extraordinary real-world demonstration of the flexible, adaptable world of modern technology, it was recently revealed that some Mars Rover robotic tasks were being run not from the Jet Propulsion Lab but from a second floor office in a gentrified section of lower Manhattan.[8] The landing of the Mars Rover took place shortly after Uranus entered Pisces, a synchronous signal that the journey of inventive Uranus through Pisces was going to be very robotic.

One of the astrological "signatures" of the present planetary placements of Uranus in Pisces and Neptune in Aquarius is that there is a tendency for technology to spread, seeping into all corners of the culture. In order for this to happen, technology has to become affordable. That is what happened with the personal computer, the digital camera—and will happen, very soon, with robots. One can envision the day when these Mars robots, with prices reduced to Wal-Mart levels, will pick up dust bunnies instead of red rocks or rake leaves instead of the Martian surface. If you don't believe the Mars Rover will ever become available at the mall, just remember: the multi-million-dollar mainframe computer eventually became the five-hundred-dollar desktop PC.

Underwater Robots

We will see more and more robots performing underwater. Pisces is a water sign. With Uranus in Pisces, we will see lots of technology involving water or liquid. Mitsubishi has developed a robotic fish for use in aquariums. It can be designed to look and behave exactly like extinct or rarely-seen fish such as the coelacanth.[9] Fish robots will also be used to search huge areas of the ocean, looking for pollution or making deep-sea maps. Robots the size of lobsters, able to mimic crustacean behavior, are being developed for eventual applications as marine minesweepers and deep-sea data gatherers.

Health Care and Robots

The medical field will continue to find new ways to use robotics. Pisces is the sign most associated with medicine and health care. Surgeons already use robots to make precise, minute incisions. Robots will also be used for such operating-room tasks as holding instruments and positioning limbs.[10] Coronary bypass surgeries have even been completed by a surgeon using three robotic arms (known as the da Vinci System, named after Leonardo da Vinci, who designed the first robot) inserted through small incisions in the chest. This area of robot technology will continue to accelerate and amaze.[11]

Robots will also be used as replacements for operating-room nurses, handing scalpels and sponges to the surgeon.

Prosthetic arms, legs, and hands will employ sophisticated robotic technology. Sadly, the battlefield is driving this field of robotics, too: a high number of Iraq War military personnel need prosthetics and rehabilitation for limbs that have been lost in combat.

Invisible Bots

Neptune can make things hard to see or notice. Many robots will operate almost invisibly, escaping our notice. We already have invisible robots hidden in home computers, where they scurry around in our hard drives. They are nicknamed bots and, among other nefarious tasks, they spy on our computers, help to activate pop-up ads, and clog up valuable space. Internet search engines like Google also use bots for a more benign purpose, trolling the Internet for web pages to add to search lists. Look for these invisible robots, both the good and the bad, to multiply in quantity and applications.

Robots, Ben Franklin, and Security

As noted in chapter 7, beginning in 2008 our cultural experiences will have many of the characteristics associated with one of America's founders, Benjamin Franklin. He was a down-to-earth inventor of utilitarian devices and would most certainly have welcomed robots—as long as they were practical and helped people to do a better job. Franklin invented bifocals, as well as the long arm used to reach books on high shelves. Like Franklin's sensible eighteenth century inventions, affordable and practical gadgets—including small robots—are set to hit the consumer market. An aging population will welcome

Robots: Astrology Background

Not only are Neptune and Uranus in mutual reception, but, in early 2006, Uranus squared the U.S. Uranus, and in 2008 it will oppose the U.S. Neptune. We have to go back to the early 1960s to find a similar pattern. Neptune is what we idealize and Uranus is the planet of invention. When Pluto in Capricorn is added to the mix, we get invention of small, helpful devices.

the utility of labor-saving robots that can perform simple tasks, such as cleaning the bathtub and sweeping the sidewalk.

We will soon begin to experience widespread and dramatic transformations of our world. Robots will be used for national security and border patrols. Driverless robot vehicles and drone aircraft will patrol the U.S. borders, an area of heightened concern since the terrorist attacks of September 11, 2001. Driverless utility vehicles may eventually be used for homeland border security.[12]

Honda has developed a robot named Asimo, whose name relates to the Japanese word for "leg." Asimo can run, dodge people, shake hands, and will soon be able to perform light errands such as delivering office mail. Eventually, we may see a sub-population of Asimos doing all the menial tasks robots did in the movie *I, Robot.*[13]

Look for robots to continue growing in popularity and then hit the big time consumer market in 2008 or slightly before. They may not all have humanoid personalities like R2-D2 from *Star Wars,* but with the media's help we'll love them anyway.

It's a Digital, Digital World: The Future of Music and Movies

One of the biggest effects of Uranus in Pisces will continue to be the explosive growth and new developments in movies and other forms of electronic entertainment. Pisces has to do with the cinema and music, while Uranus is projection and new technology.

Although the first movie technology was developed in the 1890s, movies did not flower as widespread popular entertainment until the 1920s—the last time that Uranus was in Pisces.

Uranus is a planet linked through myth with the blockbuster movie components of sex and violence. He was an R-rated sky god who performed his own special effects. According to the Greek creation myth, Uranus was castrated by one of his own sons. The blood of Uranus fell amongst the waves lapping on the shore, mixing with the salt water froth. Out of this mixture of blood and foam, Aphrodite—the glamorous goddess of beauty—was born.

Early cinema embodied the sky god very much like today, projecting sex and violence up close and personal on the screen. Although mild by today's standards, these excesses caused political reactions that reverberate through the present movie rating system and periodic calls for restraint in movies. The sky god component of Hollywood—displaying sex and violence—is a theme that has continued unabated down through the present. Movie comedian Fatty Arbuckle, for example, was a major star of the 1920s who was charged with the salacious death of a young starlet. Kenneth Anger's 1975 book *Hollywood Babylon* showed how an off-screen celebrity movie culture has often lost its connections with reality. There was a strong political movement to reign in movies of the 1920s that were thought to be too steamy and violent. Celebrity scandals and movie excesses finally resulted in the Hays Code, a movie-content control system created in 1930 at the end of Uranus' passage through Pisces.

The Sky God Today

Once again, we are in the midst of a movie revolution, this time made possible through digital technology. To some, there appears to be a growing lack of control over the directions of this new technology. Digital movies are easily reproduced and sold in violation of copyright laws. Sex and violence seem pervasive in many popular films, and digital pornography seeps into previously innocent corners of culture. When Pluto enters Capricorn, there will be stronger government and business attempts to control the distribution of digital entertainment.

Uranus symbolizes technology and rules the computer. Gollum in the *The Lord of the Rings* movie trilogy is a product of the computer as much as of the actor, Andy Serkis, who was wired and digitally connected to play him. The seamless merging of the real and the computer-generated has created a whole new world of possibilities in movies.

The *Lord of the Rings* movie trilogy was a Neptune in Aquarius phenomenon, created just as much on a computer screen as with old-fashioned film. As noted earlier in chapter 11, computer art will be a dominant creative trend. The blending of live action and digital animations to form huge battle scenes in the *Lord of the Rings* trilogy foreshadows the future of movies. In the climactic battle scene in *The Return of the King,* 350,000 characters were on Pellum Field. They were almost all digital creations, yet behaved individually. The huge, towering mammoth-like creatures, called mumakil ("oliphaunts" in the original book), were actually animated cartoons seamlessly blended into the battle.[14] Like the transformation of 1920s movie sets, whole worlds can now be created through digital animation and then inserted into movies. Movie directors will no longer sit only on a large movie set, directing performers with a bullhorn. Instead, they will just as often direct from a comfortable office chair in a computer lab.

The 1920s witnessed startling new developments in movie production and new public obsessions with glamorous movie stars. Movies of the 1920s demonstrated the power of Uranus in Neptune-ruled Pisces by transporting whole audiences out of this world and into imaginary celluloid realms. The present mutual reception of Uranus and Neptune has spread digital video disc (DVD) movies into homes throughout the world. Large flat-screen display panels, surround sound, and high definition television have enabled many homes to become what the old movie palaces of the 1920s once were: Piscean theaters devoted to transporting us into another world through the use of technology.

Neptune in Aquarius has brought greater audience participation, which does not mean participating in an Internet promotion or trivia quiz, but rather reading and writing online reviews of movies, helping to rate movies for others.

The mutual reception of Uranus and Neptune has helped to put more artistic power in the hands of individuals and less under the control of large corporations. Independent moviemakers will thrive. Several female movie directors have experimented with digital media rather than film because it gives a sense of female ownership in a male-dominated medium.[15] Movie festivals showcasing independent movies have become popular. In this sense, digital movies are also an extension of the Uranus-Pluto conjunction of the mid-1960s (see chapter 14).

Digital movies are changing how movies are made and distributed, although movie theaters will continue to prosper—we need to share the experience of a movie with others, too. Digital electronics are evolving rapidly. Cell phones and wireless technology will alter the landscape in many ways. Soon, we will be able to order a movie and have it delivered to a cell phone while we are out and about. We'll be able to play the movie on a cell phone while listening on headphones, then transfer the stored movie to our computer at home, burn a DVD, and finish watching the movie on high-definition television and surround sound in our living room. Finally, we'll log on to the Internet and post a review of the movie for others to read.

Of course, there are some individuals who proudly resist all this technology. A major counter-trend will come about through a large group that defines itself by being non-technological. As noted in the Neptune in Aquarius Profile at the end of chapter 11, this placement of Neptune—as well as Uranus in Pisces—brings out culture's "different drummers." There are those who will choose to march to a different and non-digital beat.

In M. T. Anderson's futuristic novel *Feed,* a few individuals try to resist the corporate and government control of information processed directly into people's brains. *Feed* is set in a future world in which personalized webpage banner ads, instant messaging, entertainment, and movie promotions are fed directly into people's thoughts. George Orwell's *1984* forecast a similar world of technology used to control minds. An anti-technology movement will gain force as we move into the second decade of the twenty-first century.

Listen to the Music

Music will spread with digital technology. With Uranus in Pisces and Neptune in Aquarius, we are experiencing a world in which music is everywhere. The Apple iPod has enabled music to be downloaded and played wherever we are, connecting listeners in a digital world. The pervasive portability of music is a modern phenomenon, and it will continue to be a strong trend. Music also transcends and crosses borders, another quality of the mutual reception of Uranus and Neptune. World music and so-called crossover music are growing in popularity.

Uranus in Pisces Profile: Charlie Chaplin and the Silent Cinema

It is easy to lose sight of the humanity of Uranus in Pisces when we look at robots and biogenetics. However, Charlie Chaplin's beloved character of the Little Tramp, created during the last passage of Uranus through Pisces, reminds us of the human side of this placement. Describing the appeal of the Tramp, Chaplin himself noted the many-faceted nature of this character. There is something appealing in his universal optimism, a further reflection of the power of Uranus in Pisces.[16] Part of the Little Tramp's enduring attraction lies in his ability to bounce back from failure and rejection.[17] Pisces was ruled in traditional astrology by Jupiter, which can give the sign a buoyant, optimistic quality.

Pisces is all-embracing. It is the sign ruled by Neptune and is associated with underlying connections between people. Chaplin's character of the Little Tramp has universal appeal. In the iconic image of Charlie Chaplin—his spirit unbroken despite a lifetime of mishaps, jauntily walking away down an open country road—early moviegoers saw a reflection of themselves.

The 1920s, while Uranus was in Pisces, also saw great advances in movie technology and delivery. Film editing, tinting, toning, stunts, elaborate sets, and great movie palaces all came about during the 1920s.

Another silent film comedian, Buster Keaton, symbolized the newfound universal blending available through the movies. He perfected sight gags in which inanimate objects became animate and he—Keaton—became inanimate. In one movie scene, he blended with the statue of a horse, deceiving people into believing he was a part of the sculpture. He was a master of the sight gag, made possible with the movies in a way vaudeville could never allow.

The comedy of Chaplin and Keaton bore more of a resemblance to dreams than to humor. Since Pisces is the astrological sign associated with dreams and Uranus is projection, dreams are apt metaphors for the cinema of these silent clowns.

Charlie Chaplin: Astrology Background

Chaplin's Sun was in pioneering Aries. Uranus is in Chaplin's Twelfth House, and Pisces is the natural sign of the Twelfth House. The Twelfth House has many of the same qualities as does Pisces, including dreams, collective consciousness—and silence. The co-ruler of Pisces is Jupiter, a comic at heart.

In Keaton's silent classic *The General*—considered by some critics to be among the greatest movies of all time—Keaton plays a train engineer, a stoic and understated Everyman. "The General" is the name of his beloved train. The movie is a series of extended train chase sequences which, instead of growing tedious, become ever more elaborate and amazing. Keaton directed the movie and performed his own stunts. In comparing his character with Chaplin's little tramp, Keaton unknowingly provided a perfect description of a Piscean character when he said his screen persona was simply an honest workingman.[18]

Astro-Connections Activity

Headlines

Look for news about trends. Are there news stories about particular developments in digital arts, science, and technology? These areas, especially, are where the action is in trends because of the current intensity of Uranus and Neptune. Also, pay attention to entertainment technology and delivery. More and more, entertainment is mirroring life, only bigger. Wide-screen TVs, DVDs, and surround-sound theaters put home audiences right in the action. News services are always trying to stay a step or two ahead of the present and will often report trends in science, fashion, culture, and world affairs.

Make connections between news about trends and planetary cycles presented in this book. Any new discovery, invention, gadget, or mass behavior trend can be linked to planetary influences.

Endnotes

1. This section on biogenetic trends is adapted from an article I wrote for the Dec./Jan. 2005 issue of *The Mountain Astrologer*. The article was titled "Astrology and the Human Genome."
2. The finished human genome sequence was officially announced on April 14, 2003. Uranus entered Pisces on March 10, 2003.
3. Juan Enriquez, *As the Future Catches You: How Genomics and Other Forces Are Changing Your Life, Work, Health, and Wealth* (New York: Crown Business, 2001) 121. Enriquez also predicts, in *As the Future Catches You*, that the next decade will see the following industrial sectors grow: genomics, bioinformatics, nanotechnology, photonics, robotics, and entertainment.
4. Ibid., 108.
5. Alex Zarembo, "Injections Temporarily Turn Slacker Monkeys into Model Workers," *The Los Angeles Times*, 12 August 2004: A1.
6. Lance Ulanoff, "UNECE Predicts Robot Explosion." *PC Magazine*, 20 October 2004, http://www.pcmag.com/article2/0,1759,1681016,00.asp (accessed 22 August 2006).
7. "Military Robots to Get Swarm Intelligence," NewScientist.com, 25 April 2003, http://www.newscientist.com/article.ns?id=dn3661 (accessed 22 August 2006).

8. Kenneth Chang, "Martian Robots, Taking Orders from a Manhattan Walk-Up," *The New York Times*, 7 November 2004: 1.

9. "Robot Fish to Resurrect Fossils," BBC News, 25 February 1999, http://news.bbc.co.uk/1/hi/sci/tech/286345.stm (accessed 22 August 2006).

10. Michelle Meadows, "Robots Lend a Helping Hand to Surgeons," in the U.S. Food and Drug Association online magazine *FDA Consumer*, Volume 36, Number 3, May–June 2002, http://www.fda.gov/fdac/features/2002/302_bots.html (accessed 23 August 2006).

11. Gary Singh, "The Robot Will See You Now." *Metro*, 6–12 October 2004, http://www.metroactive.com/papers/metro/10.06.04/scalpelbots-0441.html (accessed 22 August 2006).

12. "Unusual Pair Team Up on Battle-Ready Robot" MSNBC News, 25 October 2004, http://www.msnbc.msn.com/id/6718239 (accessed 22 August 2006).

13. "Honda Robot Learns to Jog," MSNBC.com, 15 December 2004, http://www.msnbc.msn.com/id/6718239 (accessed 23 August 2006).

14. *The Lord of the Rings* DVD, "The Appendices Part 6: The Passing of an Age: Weta Digital," dir. Peter Jackson, New Line Home Entertainment, 2004.

15. Philippa Bourke, "Taking the Digital Medium into Their Hands. Storytelling by Women Filmmakers Evolves with DV," 9 August 2002, http://www.moviesbywomen.com/articles/philippadv.html (accessed 22 August 2006).

16. Jeffrey Vance, *Chaplin: Genius of the Cinema.* (New York: Harry N. Abrams, Inc., 2003), 33.

17. Vance, 20.

18. Roger Ebert, *The General* movie review, http://www.ebertfest.com/six/general.htm (accessed 22 August 2006).

PART IV

Seeing the Big Picture: Planet Cycles and Major Trends

Truth is the shattered mirror strown
In myriad bits; while each believes
His little bit the whole to own . . .

—Sir Richard Burton, "Stanzas from the Kasidah"

The brawling of a sparrow in the eaves,
The brilliant moon and all the milky sky,
And all that famous harmony of leaves,
Had blotted out man's image and his cry.

—William Butler Yeats, "The Sorrow of Love" (written in 1894, just after the Neptune-Pluto conjunction)

CHAPTER 13

A Tidal Wave: The Neptune-Pluto Conjunction

NEPTUNE	PLUTO
Idealized	Powerful
Visions	Intense
Fashion	Obsessive
Drugs	Exposing
Illusive boundaries	Transforming
Merging	Extreme
Worship	Resourceful
Ephemeral	Probing
Glamorous	Secretive
Image	
Transcendence	
Yearning	

It's one thing to link astrology to retail fashions or popular music—trends with a limited shelf life. But there are other longer-range social and cultural trends that act like tidal waves, sweeping everything in their paths and inexorably shaping the cultural environment.

When Uranus, Neptune, or Pluto cross paths with one another, the effects on culture, society, and the world are momentous. In 1891 and 1892, Neptune and Pluto joined in the heavens for the first time in 492 years. Collective dreams and visions merged with transformation. This conjunction signaled the birth of the modern era, symbolizing gradual and far-reaching cultural changes. The aftereffects will continue to be felt for centuries.

The power of tidal waves was demonstrated for the world to see and experience on December 26, 2004, when earthquake-generated tidal waves swept ashore in Southeast Asia, killing many tens of thousands of people. Unlike regular waves, which are only on the surface of the water, tidal waves run the whole vertical depth of the water, from the surface to the ocean floor. When they hit land, they are, depending on the configuration of the shoreline, often experienced as a rapidly rising tide that reaches a height that can sometimes be three stories above sea level. The tidal wave, like the Neptune-Pluto conjunction, overpowers everything in its path.

The Neptune-Pluto conjunction is also like a shattered mirror. If we try to put the pieces of a shattered mirror back together again, our reflection will still be fractured and dislocated. When Neptune meets Pluto every half-millennium, a mirror is shattered and we cannot see ourselves in the same way ever again, no matter how carefully we try to glue the shards of the mirror back together.

The Neptune-Pluto conjunction took place in multifarious Gemini, making it seem like a prism refracting light. The single beam of civilization suddenly had dangled in front of it a giant prism that broke the single light into a dancing, sparkling spectrum. The prismatic effect of this conjunction in Gemini showed the fragmenting of old hierarchies. It symbolized that we are destined to be transformed by valuing diversity.

The Neptune-Pluto conjunction represented the modernist revolution in art and culture, the break from the past. It gave birth to the individual quest for spiritual meaning in life. Fragmentation, alienation, and a sense of dislocation were the negative manifestations of the Neptune-Pluto conjunction.

The Neptune-Pluto Conjunction: Astrology Background

The Neptune-Pluto conjunction took place at the exact degree as Uranus in the U.S. horoscope, which gave the conjunction extra intensity in the areas ruled by Uranus (see chapter 9) in the United States. This intense influence in areas like technology will continue for centuries.

Neptune-Pluto Today: Astrology Background

After conjoining in 1892, Neptune began pulling away from Pluto until, in 1950, they were 60 degrees apart, forming a sextile, an angle that facilitates intelligent and inventive expressions. In astrology, a sextile fosters an eagerness for new learning experiences. It has some of the same qualities as the sign of

Gemini,[1] the sign where Neptune and Pluto conjoined in 1893. This sextile between Neptune and Pluto is a phenomenon that will continue off and on until 2032. It helps to explain a half-century of erosion of community coincident with the rise of television, as noted in Robert Putnam's book *Bowling Alone*. It symbolizes the fragmentation of our world and our lives in many ways. We have moved away from centralized control and towards greater individual autonomy in many areas of life.

Modernism

Artists and poets are among the first to symbolically communicate vast cultural transformations, and the Neptune-Pluto conjunction can be seen in a trip to an art museum. The Impressionist art of Monet and Renoir, two late-nineeteenth century artists, was done just before the conjunction. Mary Cassatt painted realistic portraits just as the Neptune-Pluto conjunction was taking place. Compare the work of these artists with Pablo Picasso's early-twentieth century Cubism or Wassily Kandinsky's early abstractions. Both Picasso and Kandinsky were, in a sense, working with the shards of a shattered mirror and trying to find new ways to view the fragmented reflection.

Poetry also reflected the Neptune-Pluto conjunction. Walt Whitman, who died during the conjunction, wrote a far different type of poetry than did T. S. Eliot, whose writing came after the Neptune-Pluto conjunction. Whitman, writing in the post–U.S. Civil War period, employed a full, rich voice in poems such as "I Hear America Singing" and "O Captain! My Captain!" Contrast Whitman's poems with the sense of dislocation in Eliot's "The Wasteland" (1922), a landmark of modern poetry.[2] Although written almost three decades after the Neptune-Pluto conjunction, "The Wasteland" captured the twentieth century's growing sense of cultural and spiritual alienation.

The certainty of Alfred Lord Tennyson's clarion Victorian call "to strive, to seek, to find, and not to yield"[3] was replaced with Eliot's desperate and metaphoric pub keeper's cry in "The Wasteland" that closing time had arrived.[4]

In 1902, just ten years after the Neptune-Pluto conjunction, Joseph Conrad published *Heart of Darkness*. It was a truly modern piece of literature, using language and syntax to mirror the disintegration of the human psyche. Commenting on the tale about to unfold, the speaker in the novel says:

> *The meaning of an episode was not inside like a kernel but outside, enveloping the tale which brought it out only as a*

> *glow brings out a haze, in the likeness of one of these misty halos that, sometimes, are made visible by the spectral illumination of the sunshine.*[5]

These lines capture the essence of Neptune's influence in this novel, which is also Plutonian in its description of a riverboat voyage into the moral heart of darkness.

To say that the Neptune-Pluto conjunction created this break with the past, however, would be an oversimplification. Revolutionary art and literature evolves out of the past. However, one of the characteristics of this conjunction is breaking away from dependence on others, a powerful trend that has continued unabated in many fields, not just art, throughout the twentieth century and into the twenty-first.

A major astrological alignment like the Neptune-Pluto conjunction works in surreptitious, slow ways to undermine the past. It only looks clear to us from the vantage point of history and, from the perspective of the twenty-first century, the birth of modernism seems to have clearly begun at the transition from the nineteenth to the twentieth centuries.

Even photography experienced a shift to modernism. Photographers, like paint artists, experimented with different ways of seeing the world. Works created by photographic artists like Alfred Stieglitz and Lewis Hine bore little resemblance to more traditional portrait photos. These modernist photographers presented a visual world that often did not show what the eye actually saw. Later photography by Man Ray and László Moholy-Nagy banished or manipulated forms in abstract ways.[6]

The modernism of the Neptune-Pluto conjunction eventually led to a place where art and viewer were brought into the same field. Minimalist art included objects like *6 x 6 Den Haag Steel Lock*, a mat of steel plates arranged to form a black square. It was meant to be walked on in a museum.[7] The boundaries were broken down and art was transformed so that the museum visitor could merge with the art. This same dynamic extended into other performance art fields such as theater.

Fragmentation

The Neptune-Pluto conjunction in Gemini symbolizes the ongoing fragmentation of culture. This fragmentation can be seen in the growth of a consumer culture that tailors products more and more to individual needs. Mass marketing has slowly become niche marketing.

Television has followed this trend toward fragmentation. Cable television allows small, more focused channels to appeal to narrow markets. Ownership of these markets, however, may end up in the hands of a few, giving the Neptunian illusion of choice. The Neptune-Pluto conjunction is the intersection of marketing, control, dreams, and transformation. In John Steinbeck's short novel *The Pearl*, the pearl buyers appear to compete with one another but their businesses are all owned by the same person—a monopoly in disguise.

Neptune-Pluto Profile: Martha Graham

Several notable individuals were born during the Neptune-Pluto conjunction. These include Aldous Huxley, author of *Brave New World* and explorer of consciousness in *The Doors of Perception*. Poet E. E. Cummings was born during this conjunction; in poems such as "anyone lived in a pretty how town," Cummings turned the page into a prism that refracted the light of words. Alfred Kinsey took sex out of the Victorian bedroom and put it into the lab. The Neptune-Pluto conjunction also has a strong element of spiritual evolution and expression. Paramahansa Yogananda, who was also born at the time of the Neptune-Pluto conjunction, brought Eastern spirituality to the West.

Paramahansa Yogananda: Astrology Background

Yogananda had the Neptune-Pluto conjunction exactly in his Tenth House of career: his work was to bring spiritual transformation into others' lives.

Another wonderful example of the spiritual expression of the Neptune-Pluto conjunction was dancer and choreographer Martha Graham, one of the creators of modern dance. Martha Graham's dance was a true blend of the spiritual and transformational. The conjunction's powerful placement in her horoscope gave it the capacity to ripple and surge through her body in dance.

The Graham technique of modern dance involved her belief that the body's natural center of gravity was not the base of the spine, but rather the pelvic area. Her dance movements, therefore, are dislocating thrusts from that center.

They are characterized by contractions of the body into the pelvic area, followed by a release of physical energy from that point. This release of energy was accompanied naturally by outward thrusting of the arms, hands, fingers, legs, feet, and toes. The dancer's body exploded like a supernova. Martha Graham could have been speaking of the Neptune-Pluto conjunction when she wrote that she "tried to develop the body as a pulse, a central vibration."[8] She also commented that she felt God was expressing divine energy through her body.[9] Graham said of her dancing that she wanted to break away from the past emphasis in dance on beautiful, fluid movements. Instead, she wanted the body to be an expression of inner meaning.[10]

This style of choreography can be seen in the 1979 movie musical *Hair*. The exuberant dancing in *Hair* was choreographed by Twyla Tharp, a famous choreographer and student of Martha Graham's dance school.

Martha Graham's dances also dealt with social problems and global issues. This type of artistic activism was a result of the Neptune-Pluto conjunction's blending of art and transformation. She refused to dance at the 1936 Olympic Games in Hitler's Berlin. She also created a dance that made a statement against imperialism and choreographed another about the Spanish Civil War. "Primitive Mysteries" was based on the American Indian and "Frenetic Rhythms" employed Mexican traditions. Her dance conveyed the multiplicity of Gemini, the sign where the Neptune-Pluto conjunction took place.

Martha Graham reawakened a contact with sacred dance that had been lost through both civilized ballet and folk dance. Her dancing was connected more to pagan ritual than to the flowing, diaphanous fabric and gentle movements of *Swan Lake*.

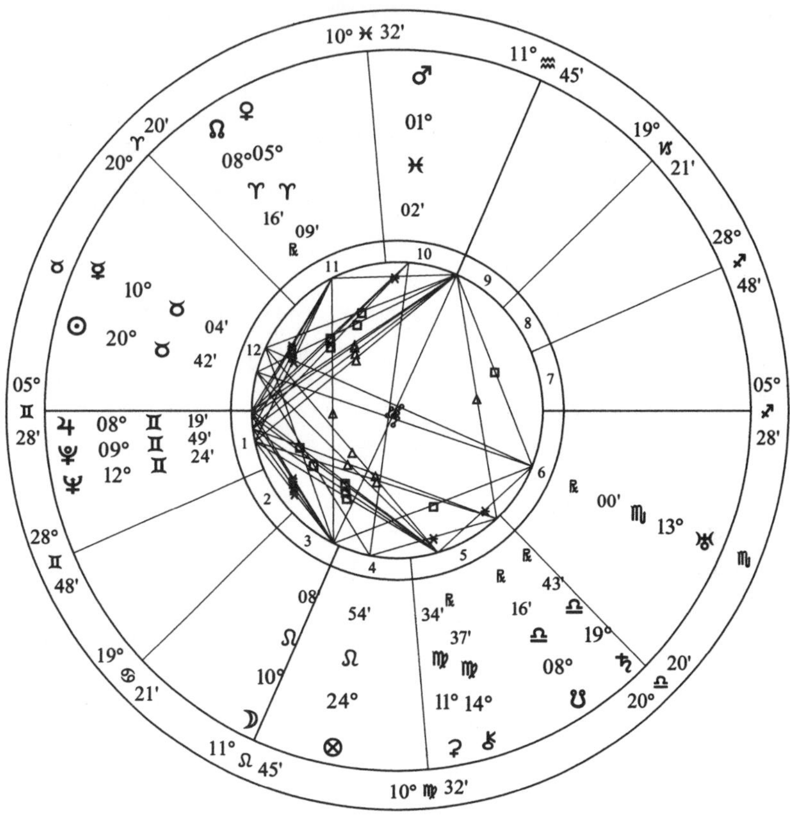

Martha Graham
May 11, 1894 / 6:00 AM EST
Pittsburgh, Pennsylvania / Placidus houses

Martha Graham: Astrology Background

Martha Graham also had Jupiter added to the Neptune-Pluto conjunction, giving her persona an added element of physicality and spiritual performance. All three—Jupiter, Neptune, and Pluto—were powerfully placed in her first house, giving the conjunction a strong physical expression.

Astro-Connections Activity

Gallery Walk

Art museums are great places to see firsthand the power of astrological cycles. Next time you visit a museum, look for the influences of major astrological cycles. You can also do the same thing by looking at art reproductions in books. Most art museums also have an extensive virtual online display, accessible through the Internet, of paintings and sculptures. Look at art before, during, and after the Neptune-Pluto conjunction. The Uranus-Pluto conjunction, discussed in the next chapter, also coincided with significant transformations in art.

Endnotes

1. Bil Tierney, *Dynamics of Aspect Analysis: New Perceptions in Astrology* (Sebastopol, California: CRCS Publications, 1983), 18–21.
2. T. S. Eliot, "The Wasteland," *The Complete Poems and Plays, 1909–1950* (San Diego, California: Harcourt Brace & Company, 1980), 38.
3. Alfred Lord Tennyson, "Ulysses," *The Norton Anthology of English Literature: Fifth Edition*, ed. M. H. Abrams (New York: W. W. Norton & Company), 1110.
4. Eliot, 42.
5. Joseph Conrad, *Heart of Darkness* (New York: W. W. Norton & Company, 1988), 9.
6. "Photographers of Genius at the Getty: March 16–July 25, 2004," The J. Paul Getty Museum exhibition brochure.
7. Richard Lacayo, "Blunt Objects," *Time*, 24 May 2004: 75–76.
8. Janet Lynn Roseman, *Dance Was Her Religion: The Sacred Choreography of Isadora Duncan, Ruth St. Denis, and Martha Graham* (Prescott, Arizona: Hohm Press, 2004), 133.
9. Roseman, 161.
10. "Martha Graham," *American Masters* PBS television series online database, http://www.pbs.org/wnet/americanmasters/database/graham_m.html (accessed 22 August 2006).

CHAPTER 14

Seeing Paisley: The Uranus-Pluto Conjunction

. . . and for those trembling stars . . . they made my heart tremble, my veins glow when I viewed them.

—Charlotte Brontë, *Jane Eyre*

URANUS	PLUTO
Quirky	Powerful
Prophetic	Intense
Rebellious	Obsessive
Revolutionary	Exposing
Explosive	Transforming
Inventive	Extreme
Objective	Resourceful
Technology	Probing
Utopian	Secretive
Quickening	
Projecting	

In 1965, Uranus and Pluto donned granny glasses and ankle bells, conjoining for the first time in 115 years. The immediate effects of this conjunction were felt for the next three years, but decades later we still continue to experience the revolutionary cultural influences of this planetary pairing. When the energies of Uranus and Pluto combine, social transformation happens at the speed of a psychedelic light show.

When the Uranus-Pluto conjunction took place, the world experienced a culture shock. Mark Kurlansky writes that the issues may have been different in different countries, but that people everywhere were united in a desire to rebel. This urge sprang out of profound alienation and distrust of authority.[1] From the Paris student rebellions to anti-Vietnam War marches in the United States, the Uranus-Pluto conjunction's effects were felt everywhere in the mid-1960s as a wave of rebellion swept the world.[2]

"Flower Power": Astrology Background

Shortly after the Uranus-Pluto conjunction took place, Uranus began to cross over Neptune in the horoscopes of many young adults. This gave a big astrological boost to the late 1960s blossoming of "flower power."

Four Powerful Uranus-Pluto Trends

Aside from its immediate cultural impact, the powerful heavenly pairing of Uranus and Pluto—the paisley conjunction—has given us some equally powerful long-term trends:

- Computers, technology, and mass media have pervaded modern culture.
- Feminism and the elevation of female consciousness have profoundly influenced society.
- Counterculture and resistance to authority grew out of the Uranus-Pluto conjunction.
- Multiculturalism and a more pluralist social fabric were first woven in the 1960s.

These four major trends are destined to continue to develop and grow.

Computers, Technology, and Media

The personal computer's foundation was laid in the 1960s when large and expensive mainframe computers were being purchased by the government and large corporations. With the development of new computing languages and micro-computing chips, coinciding with the Uranus-Pluto conjunction, the computer was poised to take off in a way few could have predicted. Only a few visionary engineers saw that the power of a room-sized computer would soon be harnessed to fit snugly on an office desk.

Technology grabbed music by the horns—or, rather, guitar strings—in July 1965, when Bob Dylan went electric with his folk music at the Newport Folk Festival. Later that year, Dylan sent shockwaves through the youthful folk music scene when he released his first electric album, *Bringing it All Back Home*. From then on, rock music was heavily amplified and often included special studio effects, adding technology to the music. In mid-1967, while the Uranus-Pluto conjunction was still very close, the Beatles performed the first live television satellite music concert, singing "All You Need Is Love" for a worldwide audience.

The British rock group Pink Floyd personified the electric Uranus-Pluto conjunction. Pink Floyd is most famous for *Dark Side of the Moon*, an album that was on *Billboard*'s Top 200 for an amazing fifteen years. When Pink Floyd made their debut on October 12, 1965, at the Countdown Club in London, Uranus and Pluto were aligned exactly together. For their earliest concerts, Pink Floyd used advertising appropriate for a Uranus-Pluto rock group, relying on guerilla ads—flyers that had been pasted up on station walls in the London Underground. A counterculture newspaper, the *International Times*, also promoted their concerts.

Pink Floyd's 1965 and 1966 music concerts featured a psychedelic light show. The light show consisted of oil slides projected on the stage and a large screen next to the stage in a display of ever-changing kaleidoscopic colors. They also showed an avant-garde, soundless Luis Buñuel movie.

The early music of Pink Floyd was throbbing, heavy with bass, descending chords, and filled with primitive space-age electronic echoes and reverberation. "Interstellar Overdrive" consisted at one point of a repetitive series of plucked guitar strings that soon dissolved into an aural mélange of abstract jazz-like noise. "Astronomy Domine" opened with a noise that sounded like Morse code. They made odd jungle-bird vocal sounds into the microphones at the opening of a song called "Pow R. Toc H"—a title that bears an uncanny resemblance to much of our current linguistic loosening with digital names and language.

Pink Floyd's music was experimental and electronic—a forerunner of the more recent digital music revolution. The light show was early multimedia. Although the current transits of Uranus and Neptune have pushed electronics to the forefront of our modern technological revolution, the Uranus-Pluto conjunction laid the foundation for the multimedia explosion of home entertainment, cellular phones, iPods, and surround-sound movie theaters.

Television in the mid-1960s made the world into a Uranus-Pluto "global village." In a world before twenty-four hour satellite broadcasts, an overseas news story televised the same day it was filed brought an immediacy to our world as never before. The Vietnam War was brought into living rooms during dinner on the six o'clock news. Today we take the reporting of breaking news stories for granted, but in the mid-1960s it awakened a visceral connection to the war, much like we experience today when television covers disasters live and unfiltered.

Videotape and live satellite transmissions, although in their infancy, were just starting to make an impact. A live broadcast from someplace like the Berlin Wall was news in itself, even if nothing was actually happening there.

Politicians soon realized that they could get noticed a lot more quickly on television if they talked louder than anyone else. Others who represented special-interest groups also found that vocal volume brought television cameras.

Feminism

The Uranus-Pluto conjunction of the mid-1960s was in the sign of Virgo, a sign associated with pre-Christian goddess worship.[3] Pluto was in Virgo from 1958 until 1972, and this by itself symbolized the raising of feminine consciousness. The conjunction created conditions for the loosening of Judeo-Christian patriarchal constraints. When Uranus and Pluto joined in Virgo, there was a quickening transformation of female consciousness, although the treatment of women in the 1960s seems arcane by today's more liberated standards. Most organizations back then were run by men and even liberal counterculture groups tended to relegate women to subservient roles. And yet, the stirrings of feminism were clear.

In the mid-1960s, the struggle over women's reproductive rights took on a heightened intensity. In 1963, Betty Friedan wrote *The Feminine Mystique*, which questioned the traditional role of women as housewives and mothers. The book sold over three million copies. In 1966, Friedan helped found the National Organization for Women.

Indira Gandhi in India and Golda Meir of Israel emerged as powerful female leaders.

There were also strong indications of feminism during the previous Uranus-Pluto conjunction of 1850–1851. Charlotte Brontë's novel *Jane Eyre* was published in 1847 and introduced one of the first strong female protagonists in literature. Jane Eyre embodied feminine assertiveness. In the context of Victorian England, it was a shock when Jane Eyre commented on gender roles:

> *[W]omen feel just as men feel; they need exercise for their faculties, and a field for their efforts as much as their brothers do . . . it is narrow-minded in their more privileged fellow-creatures to say that they ought to confine themselves to making puddings and knitting stockings . . .*[4]

Born almost a century after *Jane Eyre* was published, singer Janis Joplin would not at first seem to be an overt feminist, and she never made women's rights her personal cause. She was twenty-seven years old when she died of a drug overdose. However, she had several astrological indicators associated with feminine assertiveness and goddess worship displayed in her horoscope.

In the mid-1960s, Janis Joplin was the lead singer for a rock group called Big Brother and the Holding Company. Her performances were electrifying. Wearing a flowing, colorful blouse and loose purple pants, she stood knees slightly bent, head thrown back at the microphone, and stamped the stage with her feet while she first whispered and then shrieked the words to "Ball and Chain." Her hair was long and wild, and she danced as she sang. She was a personification of the revolutionary feminine power being symbolically unleashed through the Uranus-Pluto conjunction in Virgo.

Janis Joplin: Astrology Background

Janis Joplin was a Capricorn Sun. Capricorn is an earth sign and Janis Joplin's music was grounded in the blues. She had a strong Mercury-Pluto opposition in her horoscope, making her a powerful communicator. Most notably, she had Pallas Athena and Ceres in her First House. Pallas Athena in Greek mythology was the goddess of wisdom and the equal of men. Ceres, or Demeter, was the goddess of grain and bountiful harvests, appropriate for Joplin, who came to prominence during the Uranus-Pluto conjunction in Virgo, the sign of the harvest, and was also an alcoholic who liked to drink "grain." Ceres is the earth mother.

Counterculture and Resistance to Authority

In 1965, the Watts section of Los Angeles exploded in urban rioting. The world seethed in protest and anger in the mid-1960s. A generation gap made the youthful anger all the more palpable. Civil rights protesters in the South, student protesters in Paris, anti-Vietnam War protesters in Berkeley, and Black Panther protesters in New York all added up to a powerful movement. The echoes of these social upheavals can be felt today when placard-carrying protesters gather on the National Mall in Washington or when a hit movie documentary lambastes America's Iraq War policies.

The 1960s term "counterculture" is a perfect description because a number of people were openly rebelling against culture. Some young people burned draft cards or moved to Canada as a form of protest against the Vietnam War. Men's hair lengths grew and grew. Fashions were likewise rebellious. Masters and Johnson's *Human Sexual Response*, a clinical study of human sexuality, topped the bestseller lists as Uranus and Pluto met and, presumably, exchanged celestial phone numbers.

The Uranus-Pluto conjunction marked a new phase in the nation's movement towards a more pluralistic, multicultural society. The Civil Rights Act and Voting Rights Act were both passed by Congress in the mid-1960s, ending centuries of segregation in the South. Motown music brought African-American performers to white turntables everywhere.

Uranus-Pluto Profile: The Warlocks

If you wanted to see the future on May 5, 1965, it was playing at Magoo's Pizza Parlor in Menlo Park, near San Francisco. It was a band was called the Warlocks and they looked like male witches—especially the electric organ player, a stout, black-leather-jacketed, outlaw biker with long, thick, dark hair. One of the guitar players had a smoldering intensity and wore black motorcycle boots and his hair bristled onto his shoulders. The Warlocks were the un-Beatles.

There were no special effects and the lights were pizza-parlor bright. Nobody in the rapt, standing-room-only audience seemed to be ordering pizza. Who cared about cheese and pepperoni with music like this? Young people spilled out onto the Santa Cruz Avenue sidewalk.

The music was raw rock and roll—bluesy, gnarly, and tough. It was loud and made people want to move. There was, in the rough guitar chords and the smell of pizza ovens, the winding up of an age and the glimpse of a possibility. It was the moment when a generation was about to step into the transforming power of a momentous astrological conjunction.

Naturally, many who heard the Warlocks play were perplexed and mildly distressed when several weeks later a rumor spread that the band had changed its name to the odd and abstract-sounding Grateful Dead.

The merging energies of Uranus and Pluto marked an explosion in psychedelic drug use, paisley fashion, granny glasses, and daisy stickers. However, some did not survive the experience. There is a darker side to even the most liberating of astrological conjunctions. Ron "Pigpen" McKernan, the Grateful Dead's organist, died from alcohol abuse in 1973, and guitarist Jerry Garcia died in a drug treatment center.

In 1965, when revolutionary Uranus aligned with transformational Pluto, the doors of the future were thrown open. A rock-and-roll evening at Magoo's Pizza Parlor was just an early glimpse of how popular culture was about to be transformed by the incredible power of the cosmos.

An audience stood transfixed by music played by men with a pagan name while overhead the stars slowly criss-crossed in a nighttime sky and the world changed forever. We don't always feel connected in this world, and astrology is about re-establishing the ancient bond between heaven and earth, sky and land, our world and ourselves, or a pizza parlor and a starry California sky in 1965.

Endnotes

1. Mark Kurlansky, *1968: The Year That Rocked the World* (New York: Random House, 2004), xvii. Although Kurlansky's book title is *1968*, much of the material in his book is about the general time period of the mid-1960s—the time of the Uranus-Pluto conjunction.
2. Ibid., xvii.
3. Bernadette Brady, *Brady's Book of Fixed Stars* (York Beach, Maine: Samuel Weiser, 1998), 270; see also Deborah Houlding, "Virgo: The Maiden," Skyscript website, http://www.skyscript.co.uk/virgo_myth.html (accessed 22 August 2006).
4. Charlotte Brontë, *Jane Eyre* (New York: Bantam Books, 1981), 101.

Chapter 15

Glimpses of 2020: Jupiter Meets Saturn

Paradigm—a pattern; the generally accepted perspective at a particular time.[1]

A normally constituted truth lives, let us say, as a rule seventeen or eighteen, or at most twenty years—seldom longer. But truths as aged as that are always worn frightfully thin, and nevertheless it is only then that the majority recognizes them and recommends them to the community as wholesome moral nourishment.

—Henrik Ibsen, *An Enemy of the People*

JUPITER	SATURN
Morals	Laws
Ethics	Maturity
Law	Patience
Liberal	Integrity
Reckless	Stability
Optimistic	Limitation
Expansive	Government
Prosperity	Aging
Philosophical	Security
	Status Quo
	Boundaries
	Protection
	Detachment

Jupiter spends just one year in each sign of the zodiac, Saturn two-and-a-half years. This is enough time to influence pop music and the stock market, but it is not enough time to influence major, long-lasting trends such as alternative fuel cars or the Internet. However, Jupiter and Saturn meet in the same orbital degree every twenty years. This twenty-year planetary reunion has far-reaching effects on societies, governments, and cultures throughout the world. Jupiter is law that guarantees freedom; Saturn is law that governs and restricts. When these two planets meet, freedom collides with restriction and a new perspective emerges.

You can almost set your clock by the Jupiter-Saturn conjunction: 1940, 1960, 1980, 2000, 2020, and so on. Each span of twenty years is marked by a Jupiter-Saturn conjunction. Those who were born before the 1960s can probably visualize an approximate cultural, political, and social framework spanning the two decades of the 1960s and 1970s. The counterculture, Vietnam War, and liberal idealism of the 1960s devolved into the aftermath and cleanup efforts of the 1970s, culminating finally in a new start at the Jupiter-Saturn conjunction of 1980.

To visualize the Jupiter-Saturn conjunction, imagine two young children who are forced to share the same sandbox. One of them, Sam Saturn, is serious, lives by the rules, and is very conscious of what mother said about keeping all the sand in the sandbox. The other child, Jeri Jupiter, is carefree and happy, gaily tossing handfuls of sand in the air. The two children warily eye one another. Sam never trusted anyone who laughs too much. Jeri can't understand how "rules" and "play" can even be in the same sentence together. And yet, they have to share the same sandbox. Maybe they learn to peacefully coexist, making accommodations to each other's sandbox styles. Jeri teaches Sam some new rules, such as, "You must throw half the sand out of the sandbox." And Sam teaches Jeri how to channel all that enthusiasm into making nice sand mounds. Or, perhaps, Sam tries to restrain Jeri, they start to fight, and blood soon mixes with the sand.

Thomas Kuhn, in his groundbreaking work *The Structure of Scientific Revolutions*, explained how a paradigm shift accompanies new scientific discoveries and advances. Scientific revolutions become organized and codified, with their own sets of rules that are developed after a scientific breakthrough. The breakthrough becomes the new paradigm, or accepted way of seeing something, until the next scientific revolution, when the cycle begins all over again. Kuhn's book has had influence far beyond the scientific community. Economists, historians, and sociologists have found the theory of a paradigm shift to have many applications.

The Jupiter-Saturn conjunction symbolizes a paradigm shift in which the old rules are overthrown by events or discoveries. The old code is tossed in the dustbin. The world is seen in a new way and new rules are written, new concepts taught, new goals espoused.

One example of a recent paradigm shift is what happened after the September 11, 2001, attacks on the World Trade Center and the Pentagon. Suddenly, the nation's conception of going to the airport and boarding an airplane shifted. Gone were the halcyon days when one arrived at the airport ten minutes before the flight departed. New stringent security regulations were put in place and, for a time, passengers eyed one another nervously while boarding an airplane. The United States' view of the world suddenly shifted and a new security paradigm replaced the old.

Jupiter-Saturn Conjunction in Taurus

In 1980, the Jupiter-Saturn conjunction was in the air sign of Libra; then, in 2000, it was in Taurus, an earth sign. This signaled a sudden return, and in some cases a crash, back to earth. In 2001, the speculative-technology and stock-market bubbles burst. The NASDAQ stock index, heavy with then-popular technology and Internet stocks, began its long descent from 5,000 all the way down to just over 1,400. The vaunted and hyped Internet was co-opted by businesses, then beset with pop-up ads, viruses, worms, spam, and scams.

Taurus is strongly associated with the economy, and we will continue to see massive changes in the world economy. Many of these changes are already visible, causing unprecedented change and dislocation, both in the U.S. and in countries throughout the world. Individuals are also being affected as traditional financial protections—pensions and health insurance— are removed or transformed.

Jupiter-Saturn in Taurus: Astrology Background

The 2000 Jupiter-Saturn conjunction in Taurus was on the exact degree of the U.S. Sixth House cusp (using the Sibly chart). This indicates that health care and public health will be important national issues in the years ahead. The labor market will also be transformed. We can already see changes happening in these areas.

Jupiter-Saturn and Comedy

The Jupiter-Saturn conjunction is the perfect marker for comedy. Think of Saturn as the starched-shirt official and Jupiter as the revelers at a carnival. When they combine, the starched shirt gets doused with wine and confetti. Comic styles and types of popular humor can be traced through the different Jupiter-Saturn conjunctions:

1881: Jupiter-Saturn conjunction in Taurus—Mark Twain used the very earthy, Taurean characters of Tom Sawyer and Huck Finn to poke fun at America's gilded, uptight materialism.

1901: Jupiter-Saturn conjunction in Capricorn—Vaudeville presented the stand-up stage comedian, a person standing alone against an audience. Comedians became actors wearing personas and masks. Risqué, earthy humor began its slow and steady cultural ascent.

1921: Jupiter-Saturn conjunction in Virgo—The Little Tramp of Charlie Chaplin personified Virgoan humor. Likewise, Buster Keaton portrayed the workingman. Comic strips came into prominence. The Marx Brothers spent movie after movie deflating the pompous society matrons portrayed by Margaret Dumont.

1940: Jupiter-Saturn conjunction in Taurus—Abbott and Costello, Bob Hope, and Jack Benny all possessed the soothing and easygoing Taurean style of comedy suited for television, the new cool medium for a new nation of Ferdinands.

continued . . .

Taurus represents security and, up until the next Jupiter-Saturn conjunction in 2020, we will see great changes in our security, which will intensify when Pluto goes into Capricorn (see chapter 4), although Capricorn represents the type of security where one has to watch out for external threats. Capricorn is the lock on the safe-deposit box and the closed-circuit TV camera. Taurus is what's inside the box. Our Taurus security is being transformed. Those things that people felt they could count on as a result of hard work are being altered.

Jupiter-Saturn Fashions

Taurus is the most relaxed sign. Think of Ferdinand the bull, stopping to smell the flowers. In clothing, the current Jupiter-Saturn conjunction in Taurus has given us big and roomy clothes. Some might say it has turned us into a nation of nesting slobs, going to the video store in bedroom slippers, pajama bottoms, and a T-shirt. The trends toward loose-fitting and natural-fabric yoga clothes may also be associated with the Jupiter-Saturn conjunction in Taurus.

Shaved heads are a Taurean bullheaded look.

Jupiter-Saturn and Entertainment

The Jupiter-Saturn conjunction can be correlated with trends in entertainment. For example, *Seinfeld* was the product of the 1980 Jupiter-Saturn conjunction in Libra. *Seinfeld* was a true air show—not only on the air, but about "nothing." It was also, in true Libra form, obsessed with relationships.

Silent film star Charlie Chaplin was associated with the 1920 conjunction of Jupiter and Saturn in Virgo. Virgo is the little person, the cog in the wheel, the tramp (see the chapter 11 Astrology Profile for more on Charlie Chaplin).

The Grand Mutation

The Jupiter-Saturn conjunction changes elements every two hundred years. That is, the conjunction changes from being in, say, earth signs for two hundred years to being in air signs—a change we are starting to undergo. In astrology, this is called a Grand Mutation.[2]

The twenty-year Jupiter-Saturn conjunction was in earth signs from 1802 until 2000. In 1980, the conjunction sent a trial balloon into the air element when it was in the sign of Libra. The conjunction came back to earth in 2000, but in 2020 the Jupiter-Saturn conjunction will enter the air element to stay for close to two centuries. When the Jupiter-Saturn conjunction changes elements, the world

1961: Jupiter-Saturn conjunction in Capricorn—The clown mask of Red Skelton made him among the most popular comedians of the 1960s. Comedians like Bob Newhart developed dry, understated personas. The Smothers Brothers poked fun at the powerful and elite. Monty Python created a topsy-turvy comic world.

1980: Jupiter-Saturn conjunction in Libra—*Seinfeld* and *Friends* were two quintessential television comedies about modern relationships. *Saturday Night Live* debuted in the 1970s, but thrived during the 1980s and 1990s, becoming a cultural icon with its deft, soft-edged parodies and impersonations. *Saturday Night Live* tried to balance the scales by poking gentle fun at the rich, powerful, and self-important.

2000: Jupiter-Saturn conjunction in Taurus—Very earthy humor abounded. Movies such as *The 40-Year-Old Virgin, Austin Powers in Goldmember,* and *Meet the Fockers* featured the comedy of down-to-earth bodily functions. The easygoing style of late-night, easy-to-take, couch-potato comedy was popular.

2020: Jupiter-Saturn conjunction in Aquarius—Internet comedians will become popular. Global humor will bridge cultures. Look for great satirists to pop balloons, poking fun at grandiose ideas and schemes, inhaling the helium of inflated concepts and talking silly. We will need humor more than ever to keep us grounded.

experiences momentous and far-reaching changes. At the next Jupiter-Saturn conjunction in 2020, expect to see the curtains begin to open on a startling new world:

- We will see the end of big industrial companies. They will be replaced by "empires of the mind."[3]
- The influence of large nation-states will wane.
- We will witness a wireless, connected world in which mind will manipulate matter.
- A new renaissance of art, literature, and ideas will take place.

The Jupiter-Saturn Conjunction

1802: Virgo (beginning a new two-hundred-year cycle in earth)

1821: Aries (completing a two-hundred-year cycle in fire)

1842: Capricorn (earth)

1861: Virgo (earth)

1881: Taurus (earth)

1901: Capricorn (earth)

1921: Virgo (earth)

1940: Taurus (earth)

1961: Capricorn (earth)

1980: Libra (foreshadowing a new cycle in air)

2000: Taurus (completing a two-hundred-year cycle in earth)

2020: Aquarius (air)

. . . and continuing in air signs until about 2200

The Jupiter-Saturn conjunction in earth signs corresponds to the growth of empires. The Roman Empire prospered during a period of Jupiter-Saturn in earth signs, and it fell when this conjunction began to move into air signs. Not long after the Jupiter-Saturn conjunction changed elements from earth to air in the fourth century AD, Rome was sacked by the Visigoths.

When the Jupiter-Saturn conjunction moved into earth signs in 1800, the British Empire flourished, followed by the American military empire and the growth of corporate empires.

When the conjunction moved into an air sign—Libra—at the start of the go-go 1980s, technology and the personal computer took off. The Internet exploded in the 1990s. In keeping with the conjunction's release from earth into air, it seemed the sky was the limit. New paradigms and new economies abounded.[4] Then, in 2000, the Jupiter-Saturn conjunction was in an earth sign again—a transitional retrogression before it moves fully into air signs in 2020, where it will remain for almost two hundred years.

When the Jupiter-Saturn conjunction enters the air element in the sign of Aquarius in 2020, we can expect a new age of wireless information to take off in remarkable ways. It will feel like the steel support beams of our world have been replaced with compressed air. Many of the technological and scientific advances that have been discussed in the preceding chapters—biogenetics, robotics, cellular technology, wireless information—will accelerate in 2020.

The fact that the Jupiter-Saturn conjunction will be in Aquarius indicates that some of the greatest change will be in technology and control of the air. There will be a battle to control ideas. The copyright wars we are seeing waged in courtrooms and the digital arena are a precursor to future conflicts over the control of ideas.

Transition and change are also unsettling, producing turmoil. Aquarius is related to groups, societies, and nations—people who come together for a common good or shared interest. Beginning with the 2020 Jupiter-Saturn conjunction, there will be massive shifts in political and international alliances. The new connections that bind us together and network the globe may feel to some like cords of strangulation.

The nation or ruler who wishes to be different, who refuses to follow the crowd, will begin to stir the world. There will be a strong urge to go down a separate path. In a community of nations, this could prove dangerous.

The air element is related to the airwaves, air travel, technology, communication, and information. These will surge beginning in 2020, combining in new and unusual ways. New inventions and developments in digital technology will amaze the world. The cell phone, primarily a tool of communication, will be used as a thought-extension tool. Text messaging, picture recording, purchasing, web browsing, not to mention plain old-fashioned phone conversations—all can be done with a simple wave of the magic wand known as the cell phone. What new uses and connections will this truly individualized technology bring forth in 2020?

The Grand Mutation in 2020 will be accompanied by frenzied social and cultural obsessions. These obsessions will feel much like the Internet stock bubble of the late 1990s, and will attach themselves to advances in technology. The recent passages of Uranus and Neptune through Aquarius have given us a foretaste of what we can expect with a Jupiter-Saturn conjunction in Aquarius. However, the Jupiter-Saturn conjunction is very much related to government and institutions. We will therefore see national boundaries altered dramatically because Aquarius has to do with boundaries and their erosion. Democracy itself will experience unprecedented change.

If one looks back to 1990 and sees the changes that have since occurred, one can begin to envision the change in 2020. The Internet began its powerful cultural ascent in the 1990s (although it existed in nascent form before then), connecting the world, consumers, and individuals in new ways. This connectivity will accelerate in 2020.

Jupiter-Saturn in Aquarius: Astrology Background

Adding to the impact of the 2020 Jupiter-Saturn conjunction will be two significant factors. First, it will be at 0 degrees of Aquarius, giving the conjunction the feel of birth into a new cultural and technological world. Second, the conjunction will be within 3 degrees of Pluto—which is at 27 degrees Capricorn—in the U.S. horoscope, adding depth and intensity to the transformation. Since Pluto is in the Second House of the U.S. horoscope, expect to see great change in the U.S. economy after 2020. In 2021, Pluto will return to the same Second House degree where it was when the nation was founded, which will intensify economic transformation and restructuring.

Jupiter-Saturn Profile: William Shakespeare

In about 1600, the Jupiter-Saturn conjunction, in a Grand Mutation, moved from the water to the fire element. Shakespeare wrote his plays when the old order, symbolized by the Jupiter-Saturn conjunction, was changing. The previously static morality plays were giving way to the fluid, smoky universe of *A Midsummer Night's Dream,* in which fairies mingle with humans and love is blind.

William Shakespeare has come to be seen as a disembodied bard who may not even be who he claims to be. He might be the Earl of Oxford, or he might be Christopher Marlowe. A 2004 book by Stephen Greenblatt, *Will in*

William Shakespeare: Astrology Background

In Shakespeare's horoscope, Saturn was in the last degrees of a water sign and Jupiter was at 0 degrees of a fire sign. The conjunction was still taking place in water, but Jupiter had just moved a little ahead and out of the water sign of Cancer by the time Shakespeare was born in 1564. Shakespeare also had an exact (to the degree minute) opposition of Uranus and Neptune, so his writing also embodied many of the Uranus-Neptune qualities discussed in chapter 9. For a writer to achieve the timeless quality of Shakespeare, surviving and thriving for centuries, it is necessary for the long-range outer planets to "carry" the horoscope.

the World: How Shakespeare Became Shakespeare, looks at Shakespeare's plays, poems, and sonnets for insight into the writer. Surprisingly, there seems to be a real William Shakespeare, not an imposter, who led a life that was expressed through his writings.

Shakespeare had Jupiter and Saturn conjunct—right next to each other—in his horoscope, although he would be forty years old by the time these two planets finally conjoined in a fire sign for the first time in over five hundred years. He embodied the transitional phase of this planetary conjunction as it moved from water to fire. By looking at how this manifested in Shakespeare's life and work, we can get some idea of our collective future as we move into and through a similarly significant and rare elemental change.

When Jupiter and Saturn were positioned together in the fire sign of Sagittarius in 1603—the first Jupiter-Saturn conjunction in a new element in two hundred years—Shakespeare was at the height of his creative powers. In 1603, Queen Elizabeth I died and King James I became England's new monarch. Shakespeare wrote his great tragedies—*King Lear, Macbeth, Othello,* and *Hamlet*—around this time. In these four plays the Grand Mutation of Jupiter and Saturn is writ large. The old order has been violated and only deep transformation can chart a way through the confusion. The opening line of *Hamlet* is resonant with the existential question of Jupiter-Saturn's birth into a new element: "Who's there?"

Shakespeare took static material that was in the culture of the time and used it in metaphorical ways. For example, he took the old morality plays—in which characters had names like Vice, Riot, and Iniquity—and gave them metaphorical form, such as Richard III's spiritual grotesquerie portrayed by physical deformity. One thing stands for another. Shakespeare realized the transforming power of metaphor. The genius of Shakespeare was to take something that was rigid in culture—such as the morality plays—and transmute it into something fluid and timeless.[5] He set the stage on fire. Shakespeare " turned the dream of the sacred into popular entertainment."[6] When we experience the Grand Mutation in 2020, the static world will be transformed, and creative individuals will find ways to draw back the curtain on a stage we cannot yet see.

Shakespeare took the folk culture of his youthful upbringing in Stratford-upon-Avon, England, and transmuted it into "something rich and strange."[7] In *King Lear,* Edgar, disguised as a madman, spouts snippets of old nursery rhymes such as Shakespeare must have known from his childhood. The Athenian lovers in the woods in *A Midsummer Night's Dream* are celebrating something that looks a lot like the May festivals of Shakespeare's rural youth. Greenblatt points out that Shakespeare made a point of urbanely distancing himself from the agrarian roots of these rites.[8] This is one of the cornerstones of modern civilization—the subjugation of the primitive in favor of the cultured. And it is one of the cornerstones of the elemental change of the Jupiter-Saturn conjunction. We become ever more removed from our collective past because a change of elements is really entering a new dimension.

The water element is generally conservative and is associated with religion and religious institutions. Jupiter-Saturn in water signs indicated a society in which religion predominated. The Catholic Church, a major force in medieval European culture, was under attack. In fact, one of the forces that shaped Shakespeare was intense church conflict in England. The Jupiter-Saturn conjunction moved from water to fire just as the Protestant Reformation was "catching fire." When Jupiter-Saturn moved into the fire element, society became much more future-oriented and the fires of creative development were stoked.

In our own day and age, the Jupiter-Saturn conjunction in earth signs has brought the Industrial Revolution and vast, mighty nations. As the conjunction moves into air signs, we are entering the information age of a digital world. Just as Shakespeare's era saw the death of religion as the ruling cultural force, so will we see the death of industrial power and vast, mighty nations roaming the earth. We will instead see a new renaissance world, much as Shakespeare saw and to which he gave living, breathing form in his plays.

Endnotes

1. "Paradigm." Word Net 1.71. Princeton University, 2001. Answers.com, http://www.answers.com/topic/paradigm-1 (accessed 22 August 2006).
2. The astrologer Charles Carter, in *Introduction to Political Astrology* (Southampton, England: L. N. Fowler & Co., Ltd., 1980), calls it a Mutation Conjunction rather than a Grand Mutation.
3. Juan Enriquez, *As the Future Catches You: How Genomics and Other Forces Are Changing Your Life, Work, Health, and Wealth* (New York: Crown Business, 2001), 59.
4. Stephen Arroyo, in *New Insights in Modern Astrology* (Sebastopol, California: CRCS Publications, 1984), co-authored with Liz Greene, notes that the 1980 Jupiter-Saturn conjunction in Libra was intensified by the fact that Saturn is exalted in Libra. Exaltation is part of traditional astrology and means that a planet can express itself more fully in the sign of its exaltation. In traditional astrology, Saturn ruled Aquarius, so we can expect to see intense change beginning in 2020, when the Jupiter-Saturn conjunction is in Aquarius. In *New Insights in Modern Astrology,* the authors convey many excellent insights about the Jupiter-Saturn conjunction and its Grand Mutation.
5. Stephen Greenblatt, *Will in the World: How Shakespeare Became Shakespeare* (New York, W. W. Norton & Company, 2004), 32–34.
6. Ibid., 36.
7. William Shakespeare, *The Tempest* (New York: Pocket Books, 1961), 21.
8. Greenblatt, 40–41.

Appendix A

Planet and Sign Keywords

On the next two pages, you will find lists of planet and sign keywords. I have included only the planets (and the signs they rule) that are included as chapters in this book. Although Jupiter is not an outer planet, it forms one half of the influential and far-reaching Jupiter-Saturn conjunction (see chapter 15). For descriptions of all twelve zodiac signs, see Appendix C: Connecting with the Zodiac Signs.

I have intentionally kept the keywords general so that they can be large umbrellas for narrower concepts. You will need to "mix and match" the keywords to look for the combinations that resonate. Use your imagination. Think in broad terms. The keywords are intended to cover a multitude of possibilities. The Neptune in Aquarius keywords "egalitarian glamour" could apply to Martha Stewart as well as the *American Idol* television talent show. The Astro-Connections Activities in the book can help you to make these imaginative leaps.

Planets	Signs
PLUTO, ruler of →	**SCORPIO**
Powerful	Depth
Intense	Control
Obsessive	Secret
Exposing	Manipulation
Transforming	Emotional crisis
Extreme	Darkness
Resourceful	Survival
Probing	Hidden emotions
Secretive	
NEPTUNE, ruler of →	**PISCES**
Idealized	Escape
Visionary	Beauty
Fashion	Artistic
Drugs	Unreality
Merging	Creativity
Worship	Ambiguity
Ephemeral	Uniformity
Glamorous	Spirituality
Imagination	Compassion
Transcendence	Loneliness
Yearning	Sensitivity
Dissolving	Conspiracy
URANUS, ruler of →	**AQUARIUS**
Quirky	Ideas
Prophetic	Society
Rebellious	Internet
Revolutionary	Egalitarian
Explosive	Detachment
Inventive	Revolution
Objective	Technology
Technology	Globalization

Planets	Signs
Utopian	Public domain
Quickening	Airwaves
Projecting	Groups
Sudden awakening	
SATURN, ruler of →	**CAPRICORN**
Laws	Aging
Maturity	Parental authority
Patience	Security and control
Integrity	Sensory pleasure
Stability	Nostalgia
Limitation	Status quo
Government	Ambition
Aging	Protection
Security	Networking
Status quo	Social masks
Boundaries	Big business
Protection	Release of instinct
Detachment	
JUPITER, ruler of →	**SAGITTARIUS**
Morals	Travel
Ethics	Law
Law	Sports
Liberal	Freedom
Reckless	Religion
Optimistic	Expansion
Expansive	Promotion
Prosperity	Perspective
Philosophical	

APPENDIX B

Glossary of Terms

Aspect—A particular angle or conjunction between two planets in the horoscope.

Conjunction—A conjunction occurs when two or more planets' orbits are close to the same orbital point at the same time.

Mutual reception— When two planets "trade signs"; the planetary rulers of two zodiac signs are in each other's signs.

Outer planets—New discoveries in our expanding solar system have created the need for new definitions of the outer planets. Although this book refers to Uranus, Neptune, and Pluto as outer planets, they are "outer" mainly in the sense that they are beyond Saturn and cannot be seen with the naked eye. That is, they are outside the realm of unaided sensory perception. However, they are not the limits of our solar system. Pluto, especially, continues to evolve and seek new meaning—as both planet and powerful influence in the world. Of the objects that have been identified by astronomers in our solar system, Uranus, Neptune, and Pluto are presently considered to have the most influence over social and cultural trends. Because their orbits take longer, these planets' movements through the twelve signs of the zodiac are associated with slow social and cultural changes. Their placement in our horoscopes helps to define us as individuals, and also symbolizes our individual connections to the world. Astrologers sometimes think of Saturn as an outer planet, but more often it is considered to be the "boundary" planet.

Planetary cycles—The predictable 360 degree orbit of a planet, or a planet's regular and predictable conjunction with another planet. The predictability of planetary cycles is one reason why the popularity of astrology tends to grow during times of uncertainty. We know exactly where the planets will be tomorrow and a hundred years from now.

Retrograde—All planets except the Sun and Moon appear to slow their relative forward motion and go backwards (retrograde). Of course, the planets don't really go backwards. It just looks that way from our perspective here on planet Earth.

Transit—The movement of a planet through its orbit; the planet is "in transit."

APPENDIX C

Connecting with the Zodiac Signs

Three Modes

The twelve zodiac signs are associated with three modes and four elements. The modes are the primary ways the sign expresses itself. The terms for these three modes are: **fixed**, **cardinal**, and **mutable**.

- **Fixed** signs are stable and do not like change. Like eggshells, they have to be cracked to allow change to hatch. They are stubborn survivors and can carry a heavy load. Trends associated with fixed signs may be long-lasting or come to an end because they cannot adapt to a changing world. The obsession with remaining forever young is a fixed trend.
- **Cardinal** signs are active. They like to start things. They are first out of the starting gate, enthusiastic, and work best when there is activity, focus, and direction. They can also be impulsive and sometimes leap without looking. Cardinal trends sweep over culture, generate a lot of excitement, but may use up a lot of their energy sprinting the first lap. The hula hoop was a cardinal trend.
- **Mutable** signs thrive on change. "Mutable" has the same Latin root as the words"mutate" and "mutation," meaning "to change." Mutable signs are often curious and open, although they can be indecisive and hard to pin down. Mutable trends can sometimes just be short-lived fads or they may survive for a long time by changing and adapting new forms. Many fashion trends are mutable.

Four Elements

- The four elements are fire, earth, air, and water.
- Fire is active and attention-getting.
- Air is communication and ideas.
- Earth is stable and practical.
- Water is feeling and sensitivity.
- Fire and air are attuned to the future.
- Earth and water are sensitive to the past.

The Twelve Signs

As the planets move around the zodiac wheel, they spin a fabric of the future. Planets and signs keep their basic energies no matter how they are applied or interpreted. Whether we are looking at the astrology of a person or the astrology of a cultural trend, planets and signs still have the same basic energy. What changes is how we apply the basic meanings.[1] The keywords for Pluto can be used for personal horoscope insights as well as for events and trends. However, when astrology is applied to trends, societies, culture, and events, we need to look for broad and original applications. After all, we are trying to connect events and trends that seem to be random. Coincidences, synchronicities, and parallel events are important when using astrology to spot trends. Trends come out of mass psychology. Even advertisers, for all their ability to manipulate trends, are really just responding to social moods and psychology.

This book is concerned with the signs Capricorn, Aquarius, and Pisces. These three signs are and will be the most important for trends for quite a few years. However, since the other signs are mentioned from time to time in this book, I am providing a quick overview of each of the twelve zodiac signs. Each sign is "ruled" by a planet.

1. Aries, the ram, is a cardinal fire sign; it is ruled by Mars. A good Aries friend of mine always seemed too modest and conservative to be an Aries—until I watched her set off backyard fireworks on the Fourth of July! It was like a battle zone. Aries loves to light the fuse, stand back, and watch the snap, crackle, and hiss before a Roman candle gushes skyward in a spray of sparks. Aries can give the appearance of modesty, like Sun in Aries Charlie Chaplin.

However, it loves to light the fire of ideas, activities, and exploration. Aries can also, in true ram fashion, butt heads. It often leads, headstrong, with an impulsive idea that may or may not be a good one. It is very courageous. If I had to walk through the valley of the shadow of death, I'd want an Aries to hold my hand and walk beside me. Aries is the pioneer blazing a new trail. Feminist publisher Gloria Steinem and artist Vincent van Gogh both have the Sun in Aries.

2. Taurus, the bull, is a fixed earth sign; it is ruled by Venus. They don't come much earthier than Taurus. Taurus is the field, rich loam, fertile soil. It craves stability and things that last. It is the sign most often associated with the accumulation of wealth. Taurus can persevere through anything and shoulder any load. It can build, construct, and create something great out of the most meager materials, even if it takes a lifetime. Taurus also loves to contemplate, to be like Ferdinand and poke along, smelling the flowers. It rules the throat. Some famous singers, like Bono of the rock band U2 and Barbra Streisand, have the Sun in Taurus. Taurus represents the economy and feelings of economic well-being.

3. Gemini, the twins, is mutable air; it is ruled by Mercury. This is a youthful, lively, and energetic sign. It is the sign of the communicator and the witty intellect. President John F. Kennedy was a Gemini. Gemini enjoys change. New people, places, and ideas excite Gemini more than almost any other sign. It is ruled by Mercury and mercurial is one way to describe Gemini. They can quickly change personas. The singer Prince and poet Allen Ginsberg are/were both Geminis. Gemini also has to do with education, schools, and literature. Popular books that suddenly excite the public imagination have a Gemini quality.

4. Cancer, the crab, is a cardinal water sign; it is ruled by the Moon. Like the crab, Cancer craves privacy and appreciates the feeling of being safe inside a good, solid shell. It tends to move sideways to get to its goal. Cancer signifies our roots, our heritage. Cancer is ruled by the Moon, and in astrology the Moon represents the tidal ebb and flow of masses of people. Cancer represents the security of home and family. Land and real estate are associated with Cancer.

5. Leo, the lion, is a fixed fire sign; it is ruled by the royal Sun. Leo likes to shine and is associated with entertainers and the entertainment industry. Leo is the sign of the child, the one on whom the light of parental affection should shine bright. Leo likes to stay young and looking good. Appearances count. It is also the sign of the Dad—the Scout leader, the coach, the cool guy with a receding hairline and a slight paunch who likes to take kids to Disneyland, a ball game, or a tennis match. Or the Mom who shops for Disney collectibles on eBay and likes to dress up Barbie dolls with her daughter. Leo is the romantic, the individual, and the idealist. Leo is a Sunday afternoon. Trends having to do with the theater, sports, and gambling are associated with Leo.

6. Virgo, a virgin holding sheaves of wheat in her hands, is a mutable earth sign; it is ruled by Mercury. Virgo represents organization, engineering, and technical skill. Hardworking and diligent, it enjoys carrying an old-fashioned slide rule, a handheld calculator, or a solid tool—anything that harvests results. It is ruled by the planet Mercury and, during Pluto's passage through Virgo, the biggest celebrities were the Mercury astronauts. It facilitates and welcomes rapid change. Virgo is also the sign of the harvest; it is associated with folk culture and harvest celebrations, giving it a somewhat pagan bent. Virgo has to do with public health.

7. Libra, the scales, is a cardinal air sign; it is ruled by Venus. Libra represents relationships, balance, and harmony. It weighs and deliberates. It is also possible that by the time Libra finishes deliberating, the time for deciding has long since passed. Libra places a high premium on fairness. It has the capacity to detach and be objective, but it can also appear a bit superficial and lacking in depth. Libra likes the air of mental activity. It may excel at activities that require balancing, such as algebra or gymnastics. It is very social, enjoying the balancing act of many relationships, but this can sometimes lead Libra to get out of inner balance.

8. Scorpio, the scorpion, is a fixed water sign; it is ruled by Pluto. A survivor extraordinaire, the scorpion has survived as a species longer than any other arachnid. They are found in the desert and in the cold Andean snow. Ruled by Pluto, they like the darkness and are very secretive. Scorpios may have emotions swirling under the surface, but can look calm and untroubled on the outside. They are possessed of phenomenal regenerative powers. Scorpios can bounce back from terrible, painful experiences. They are some of the greatest students because they have an intense, almost obsessive desire to learn from mistakes and not repeat the pain of failure which they feel deeply. They are possessed of an inner reservoir of strength. They also have stingers.

9. Sagittarius, the centaur archer, is a cardinal fire sign; it is ruled by Jupiter, a god who knows how to party. Sagittarius loves the sense of freedom and release that comes from partying. Sagittarius likes to travel, whether it is in an airplane, a car, or in the pages of a book. Higher education is associated with Sagittarius. It is an adventurer, enjoying colorful new experiences, people, and places. Sagittarius is associated with the archetype of the gypsy, most often in the broader sense of a person who can be at home anywhere. It is also the sign of spirituality, the search for meaning, and religion. It can be a bit self-righteous in its beliefs, however, and when challenged, tends to be more defensive than reflective. Self-examination is usually not Sagittarius's strong suit. Sagittarius is athletic, as befits the archer with a horse's hindquarters, and many athletes have a strong Jupiter or Sagittarius in their horoscopes. It is the sign of the salesperson and the advertising promotion. Last but certainly not least, Sagittarius can have amazing perspective. When the arrow shoots straight up, it sees the sky. When the arrow reaches its apogee, it slowly turns 180 degrees and has a bird's-eye view of the earth.

10. Capricorn, the mountain goat, is a cardinal earth sign; it is ruled by Saturn. Capricorn is discussed at length in Part II of this book, but a few traits are worth noting here. Capricorn is very practical, but unlike the earthy luxury of Taurus, Capricorn is more of a rock climber, adept at spotting the best toe-hold in the crags up above the tree line where the air is thin. Capricorn is also very concerned with security, safety, and boundaries. It is comfortable in public professions because it knows how to schmooze and network. It represents national leaders and is a powerful sign where trends and events are concerned. It is the sign most closely associated with old age.

11. Aquarius, the water bearer, is fixed air; it is ruled by Uranus. Aquarius is discussed at greater length in Part III. It is an important sign today because it has to do with the airwaves and global interconnection. Things like satellite television, wireless computers, and cell phones are Aquarian. Aquarius is interested in freedom. President Franklin D. Roosevelt was an Aquarius, as was Ronald Reagan. It does not like a lot of rules and restrictions. It can also be a bit kooky and unconventional—and, in some cases, "air"-headed. Aquarius can keep going long after the fire signs have burned out, the water signs have dried up, and the earth signs have cracked. There is always plenty of air to fuel an Aquarius.

12. Pisces, the fish, is a mutable water sign; it is ruled by Neptune. Pisces is sensitive and intuitive. Like Sagittarius, it is associated with religion (in traditional astrology, both signs were ruled by Jupiter, the religious planet).

Pisces is also artistic and can reflect the world in startling and original ways. It is associated with loneliness and the unconscious. Trends that come out of the collective unconscious, as often happens with movies, are associated with Pisces. Like a fish that slips out of one's grasp, Pisces is not easy to hold. It does not do well in the air. Too much mental preoccupation is exhausting for a Pisces. They need to swim beneath the surface. Pisces also has to do with conspiracies and underground political or social movements.

Endnotes

1. Some of the cultural and social meanings I have included for the zodiac signs in Appendix C are borrowed from Charles E.O. Carter's *An Introduction to Political Astrology* (Southampton, England: L. N. Fowler & Co., Ltd., 1980).

APPENDIX D

Outer Planet Transits and Major Conjunctions Chart

Because of an astronomical phenomenon called retrograde motion, all the planets sometimes appear to slow their relative forward motion and go backwards (retrograde). Of course, the planets don't really go backwards. It just looks that way from our perspective here on planet Earth. When Pluto begins to enter a new zodiac sign, it will often appear to go backwards—retrograde—and return briefly to the previous sign for a few weeks or months. This also applies to the other outer planets. In these charts, I have highlighted the dates on which the planet entered or will enter a sign to stay for several years.

Pluto

May 26, 1914—Cancer
October 7, 1937—Leo
November 25, 1937—Cancer
August 3, 1938—Leo
February 7, 1939—Cancer
June 14, 1939—Leo
October 20, 1956—Virgo
January 15, 1957—Leo
August 19, 1957—Virgo
April 11, 1958—Leo
June 10, 1958—Virgo
October 5, 1971—Libra
April 17, 1972—Virgo
July 30, 1972—Libra
November 5, 1983—Scorpio
May 18, 1984—Libra

August 28, 1984—Scorpio

January 17, 1995—Sagittarius

April 21, 1995—Scorpio

November 10, 1995—Sagittarius

January 26, 2008—Capricorn

June 14, 2008—Sagittarius

November 27, 2008—Capricorn

March 23, 2023—Aquarius

June 11, 2023—Capricorn

January 21, 2024—Aquarius

September 1, 2024—Capricorn

November 20, 2024—Aquarius

March 9, 2043—Pisces

Neptune

May 2, 1916—Leo

September 21, 1928—Virgo

February 19, 1929—Leo

July 24, 1929—Virgo

October 3, 1942—Libra

April 17, 1943—Virgo

August 2, 1943—Libra

December 24, 1955—Scorpio

March 12, 1956—Libra

October 19, 1956—Scorpio

June 15, 1957—Libra

August 6, 1957—Scorpio

January 4, 1970—Sagittarius

May 3, 1970—Scorpio

November 6, 1970—Sagittarius

January 19, 1984—Capricorn

June 23, 1984—Sagittarius

November 21, 1984—Capricorn

January 29, 1998—Aquarius

August 23, 1998—Capricorn

November 27, 1998—Aquarius

April 4, 2011—Pisces

August 5, 2011—Aquarius

February 3, 2012—Pisces

March 30, 2025—Aries

October 22, 2025—Pisces

January 26, 2026—Aries

May 21, 2038—Taurus

October 21, 2038—Aries

March 23, 2039—Taurus

July 16, 2051—Gemini

Uranus

January 1920–March 1927—Pisces

April–October 1927—Aries

November 1927–January 1928—Pisces

January 1928–May 1934—Aries

June–September 1934—Taurus

October 1934–March 1935—Aries

April 1935–August 1941

August–September 1941—Gemini

September 1941–May 1942—Taurus

May 1942–September 1948—Gemini

September–November 1948—Cancer

November 1948–June 1949—Gemini

June 1949–August 1955—Cancer

August 1955–January 1956—Leo

February–June 1956—Cancer

June 1956–October 1961—Leo

November 1961–January 1962—Virgo

January–August 1962—Leo

August 1962–September 1968—Virgo

September 1968–May 1969—Libra

May–June 1969—Virgo

October 1968–November 1974—Libra

December 1974–April 1975—Scorpio

April–September 1975—Libra

September 1975–February 1981—Scorpio

February–May 1981—Sagittarius

May–November 1981—Scorpio

November 1981–February 1988—Sagittarius

February 1988–May 1988—Capricorn

May 1988–November 1988—Sagittarius

November 1988–April 1995—Capricorn

April 1995–June 1995—Aquarius

June 1995–January 1996—Capricorn

January 1996–March 2003—Aquarius

March–September 2003—Pisces

September–December 2003—Aquarius

December 2003–June 2010—Pisces

June 2010–January 2011—Aries

January 2011–April 2011—Pisces

April 2011–June 2018—Aries

Jupiter-Saturn Conjunction

1802: Virgo (beginning a new two-hundred-year cycle in earth)

1821: Aries (completing a two-hundred-year cycle in fire)

1842: Capricorn (earth)

1861: Virgo (earth)

1881: Taurus (earth)

1901: Capricorn (earth)

1921: Virgo (earth)

1940: Taurus (earth)

1961: Capricorn (earth)

1980: Libra (beginning a new cycle in air)

2000: Taurus (completing a two-hundred-year cycle in earth)

2020: Aquarius (air)

. . . and continuing in air signs until about 2200

Uranus-Neptune Conjunction

Note: Only the year is given; the two planets conjoined exactly, and then separated, several times during each of the years due to the phenomenon of retrogradation.

1650—Sagittarius
1821—Capricorn
1993—Capricorn
2165—Aquarius

Uranus-Pluto Conjunction

1851—Aries
1965–1966—Virgo
2104—Taurus

Neptune-Pluto Conjunction

1891–1892—Gemini
2384–2385—Gemini

APPENDIX E

Chart Data and Sources

Chapter 1—Transformational Pluto

United States Sibly Chart: 4 July 1776; Philadelphia, Pennsylvania; 5:10 PM LMT; source: Nicholas Campion, *Book of World Horoscopes* (Northamptonshire, England: The Aquarian Press, 1988) Chart 281.

Avril Lavigne: 27 September 1984; Napanee, Ontario, Canada; no birth time.

Bob Dylan: 24 May 1941; Duluth, Minnesota; 9:05 PM; source: birth certificate.

Chapter 2—Six Generations of Pluto, 1912–2008

Kurt Cobain: 20 February 1967; Aberdeen, Washington; 7:20 PM PST; source: from mother's memory.

Chapter 3—Saturn, Capricorn's Security Planet

Muhammad Ali: 17 January 1942; Louisville, Kentucky; 6:35 PM; source: birth certificate.

Diane Keaton: 5 January 1946; Los Angeles, California; 2:49 PM PST; source: *Gauquelin Book of American Charts*, 1982.

Steve Garvey: 22 December 1948; Tampa, Florida; no birth time.

Howard Hughes: 24 December 1905; Houston, Texas; 10:12 PM CST; source: Steinbrecher quotes from Hughes's uncle, Rupert Hughes, in Lois Rodden's *Astro-Data II* (American Federation of Astrologers, 1988).

Chapter 5—Blowing a Carnival Horn

Howard Stern: 12 January 1954; Long Island, New York; 1:11 PM EST; Original source unknown, although his birth data is posted on several websites.

Jim Bakker: 2 January 1939; Muskegon, Michigan; no birth time; source: various online news services.

John DeLorean: 6 January 1925; Detroit, Michigan; no birth time; source: various online news services.

J. Edgar Hoover: 1 January 1895; Washington, District of Columbia.; 7:30 AM EST; source: Lois Rodden's *Data News #13.*

Chapter 7—Ben Goes Electric: Inventing the Future

Benjamin Franklin: 17 January 1706; Boston, Massachusetts; no birth time.

Chapter 8—The Dreaming Planet: Neptune

Britney Spears: 2 December 1981; Mahon, Mississippi; 1:30 AM CST; source: from memory. (Britney Spears's visit to The Astrology Shop in London, where she had her chart calculated).

Marilyn Monroe: 1 June 1926; Los Angeles, California; 9:30 AM PST; source: birth certificate.

Fred Rogers: 10 March 1928; Latrobe, Pennsylvania; no birth time; birth date is from obituaries published after he died in 2003.

Stevie Nicks: 26 May 1948; Phoenix, Arizona; 3:02 AM; source: American Federation of Astrologers *Bulletin*, 29 March 1987.

Chapter 9—The Freedom Planet: Uranus

Bill Gates: 28 October 1955; Seattle, Washington; 10:00 PM; source: from memory, at a Microsoft function in Seattle.

James Dean: 8 February 1931; Marion, Indiana; 2:00 AM CST; source: Lois Rodden quotes biography of his life.

Nelson Mandela: 18 July 1918; Umtata, South Africa; 2:45 PM EET; source: Steinbrecher Astrological Data Collection.

Chapter 10—Visions of Utopia: The Uranus-Neptune Connection

Clara Barton: 25 December 1821; Oxford, Massachusetts; 11:52 AM LMT; source: Lois Rodden cites Barton's *Story of My Childhood in Profiles of Women: Astro-Data I.*

Chapter 11—Uranus and Neptune Star in Trading Signs

Buffalo Bill Cody: 26 February 1846; Le Claire, Iowa; 8:00 AM LMT; source: birth time is speculative in *Astro-Data II.*

Chapter 12—Future Trends with Uranus and Neptune

Charlie Chaplin: 16 April 1989; London, England; 7:24 AM LMT; source: birth certificate.

Buster Keaton: 4 October 1895; Piqua, Kansas; no birth time.

Chapter 13—A Tidal Wave: The Neptune-Pluto Conjunction

Paramahansa Yogananda: 5 January 1893; Gorakhpur, India; 8:38 PM; source: *Mercury Hour* says data came from Self-Realization Fellowship, an organization founded by Yogananda.

Martha Graham: 11 May 1894; Pittsburgh, Pennsylvania; 6:00 AM EST; source: Khaldea website, http://www.khaldea.com/charts/marthagraham.shtml (accessed 22 August 2006).

Chapter 14— Seeing Paisley: The Uranus-Pluto Conjunction

Janis Joplin: 19 January 1943; Port Arthur, Texas; 9:45 AM CWT; source: birth certificate.

Chapter 15— Glimpses of 2020: Jupiter Meets Saturn

William Shakespeare: 26 April 1564; Stratford-upon-Avon, England; no birth time; source: baptismal records.

Bibliography

Agins, Teri. *The End of Fashion: The Mass Marketing of the Clothing Business.* New York: William Morrow, 1999.

"The Amana Colonies: Utopias in America," http://www.cr.nps.gov/nr/travel/amana/utopia.htm (accessed 22 August 2006).

Anger, Kenneth. *Hollywood Babylon: The Legendary Underground Classic of Hollywood's Darkest and Best-Kept Secrets.* New York: Dell Publishing, 1981.

Asimov, Isaac. *I, Robot.* New York: Bantam Books, 1994.

Baigent, Michael, Nicholas Campion, and Charles Harvey. *Mundane Astrology.* London: Thorsons, 1995.

Barlett, Donald L. and James B Steele. *Empire: The Life, Legend, and Madness of Howard Hughes.* New York: W. W. Norton & Company, 1979.

Braudy, Leo. *The Frenzy of Renown: Fame & Its History.* New York: Vintage Books, 1997.

Brownlow, Kevin. *The Parade's Gone By.* Los Angeles: University of California Press, 1968.

Campbell, Joseph. *The Power of Myth with Bill Moyers.* New York: Doubleday, 1988.

Carter, Charles E. O. *An Introduction to Political Astrology.* Southampton, England: L. N. Fowler & Co. Ltd., 1980.

Carter, Robert A. *Buffalo Bill Cody: The Man Behind the Legend.* New York: John Wiley & Sons, Inc., 2000.

Chevalier, Jean and Alain Gheerbrant. *The Penguin Dictionary of Symbols.* Trans. John Buchanan-Brown. New York: Penguin Books, 1996.

Connolly, Sean. *Nelson Mandela: An Unauthorized Biography.* Chicago: Heinemann Library, 2001.

Cummingham, Patricia A. and Susan Voso Lab. *Dress and Popular Culture.* Bowling Green, Ohio: Bowling Green State University Popular Press, 1991.

Davison, Ronald C. *Astrology: The Classic Guide to Understanding Your Horoscope.* Sebastopol, California: CRCS Publications, 1979.

Dylan, Bob. *Chronicles: Volume One.* New York: Simon & Schuster, 2004.

Enriquez, Juan. *As the Future Catches You.* New York: Crown Business, 2001.

Friedman, Thomas L. *The Lexus and the Olive Tree.* New York: Farrar, Strauss, Giroux, 1999.

Greenblatt, Stephen. *Will in the World: How Shakespeare Became Shakespeare.* New York: W. W. Norton & Company, 2004.

Greene, Liz. *The Astrological Neptune and the Quest for Redemption.* York Beach, Maine: Samuel Weiser, 1996.

Greene, Liz. *The Outer Planets & Their Cycles: The Astrology of the Collective.* Sebastopol, California: CRCS Publications, 1996.

"History Timeline of Robotics," http://trueforce.com/Articles/Robot_History.htm (accessed 22 August 2006).

Houlding, Deborah. "Capricorn: The Goatfish." Skyscript website. http://www.skyscript.co.uk/cap_myth.html (accessed 22 August 2006).

Ives, Brian and Bottomley, C. "Avril Lavigne: More Complicated Than Most," interview transcript, http://www.vh1.com/artists/interview/1494623/12082004/lavigne_avril.jhtml (accessed 23 August 2006).

Keaton, Buster, dir. *The General.* Videocassette. Kino on Video, 1995. 75 min.

Kerr, Walter. *The Silent Clowns.* New York: Alfred A. Knopf, 1975.

Leland, John. *Hip: The History.* New York: HarperCollins Publishers, Inc., 2004.

Lewis, Peter. "And Now, R2D2 for You, Too," *The New York Times,* 6 August 1998. Available online at: http://cache.ucr.edu/~currie/R2D2&you.html (accessed 22 August 2006).

Linden, Eugene. *The Future in Plain Sight.* New York: Simon & Schuster, 1998.

Mandela, Nelson. *Long Walk to Freedom: The Autobiography of Nelson Mandela.* New York: Little, Brown and Company, 1995.

McDevitt, Theresa H. *Why History Repeats: Mass Movements and the Generations Past-Present-Future.* Ormond Beach, Florida: Venue Press, 2003.

Menand, Louis. "The Reluctant Memorialist." *The New Yorker* 8 July 2002: 55–65.

Monmonier, Mark. *Spying With Maps: Surveillance Technologies and the Future of Privacy.* Chicago, IL: University of Chicago Press, 2002.

Moore, Booth. "Airy Godmother." *The Los Angeles Times*, 23 October 1997.

Oates, Stephen B. *A Woman of Valor: Clara Barton and the Civil War.* New York: The Free Press, 1994.

O'Connor, Anne-Marie. "You're Being Watched." *The Los Angeles Times*, 26 May 2004.

Orwell, George. *1984.* New York: Signet, 1990.

Parrington, Jr., Vernon Louis. *American Dreams: A Study of American Utopias.* Providence: Brown University, 1947.

Petronius. *Satyricon*. Trans. William Arrowsmith. Franklin Center, Pennsylvania: The Franklin Library, 1959.

Roseman, Janet Lynn. *Dance Was Her Religion: The Sacred Choreography of Isadora Duncan, Ruth St. Denis, and Martha Graham.* Prescott, Arizona: Hohm Press, 2004.

Rykwert, Joseph. *The Seduction of Place: The City in the Twenty-first Century.* New York: Pantheon Books, 2000.

Schlosser, Eric. *Fast Food Nation: The Dark Side of the American Meal.* New York: Perennial, 2002.

Shakespeare, William. *Twelfth Night,* or *What You Will.* New York: Pocket Books, 1964.

Shelton, Robert. *No Direction Home: The Life and Music of Bob Dylan.* New York: Beech Tree Books, 1986.

Spotts, Peter N. "Fishing for Data." *Christian Science Monitor*, 27 November 2002. Reproduced online at http://www.csmonitor.com/2002/1127/p18s01-stct.html (accessed 22 August 2006).

Tessitore, John. *Muhammad Ali: The World's Champion.* New York: Franklin Watts, 1998.

Thearling, Kurt. "Data Mining and Privacy: A Conflict in the Making?" Originally published in *Data Storage*, 17 March 1998. Reproduced online at http://www.thearling.com/text/dsstar/privacy.htm (accessed 22 August 2006).

Thearling, Kurt. "An Introduction to Data Mining." http://www.thearling.com/text/dmwhite/dmwhite.htm (accessed 23 August 2006).

Thérèse, Saint of Lisieux. *The Autobiography of Saint Thérèse of Lisieux: The Story of a Soul.* Trans. John Beevers. New York: Doubleday Image, 1987.

Tierney, Bil. *Dynamics of Aspect Analysis: New Perceptions in Astrology.* Sebastopol, California: CRCS Publications, 1983.

Tompkins, Sue. *Aspects in Astrology: A Comprehensive Guide to Interpretation.* Boston: Element, 1997.

Vance, Jeffrey. *Chaplin: Genius of the Cinema.* New York: Harry N. Abrams, Inc., 2003.

Willett, Edward. "Future Cars," 1997. Posted online at http://www.edwardwillett.com/Columns/futurecars.htm (accessed 22 August 2006).

Wright, Paul. *Astrology in Action.* Sebastopol: CRCS Publications, 1989.

Yemma, John. "The Bionic Lobster," *The Boston Globe.* Available online at http://cache.ucr.edu/~currie/lobster.html (accessed 22 August 2006).

Yogananda, Paramahansa, *Autobiography of a Yogi.* Los Angeles: Self-Realization Fellowship, 1968.

Index

Llewellyn's New A to Z Horoscope Maker and Interpreter

A Comprehensive Self-Study Course

Llewellyn George

New and Improved: The #1 Astrology Text in the World!

The Classic Text Revised & Expanded by
Marylee Bytheriver & Stephanie Jean Clement, Ph.D.
Includes free birth chart offer.

For ninety-three years, astrologers the world over have trusted the *A to Z* as their primary textbook and reference for all major facets of astrology.

Now this famous classic enters the new millennium with a huge makeover and additions totaling more than 31,000 words. Today's generation of astrologers can benefit from Llewellyn George's timeless interpretations, along with new material by contemporary astrologer and author Stephanie Jean Clement. The expansion includes modern developments in astrology as well as a Study Guide, making *Llewellyn's New A to Z* the most comprehensive self-study course available.

0-7387-0322-2, 504 pp., 7½ x 9⅛, illus., tables **$19.95**

To order, call 1-877-NEW-WRLD

Prices subject to change without notice

To Write to the Author

If you wish to contact the author or would like more information about this book, please write to the author in care of Llewellyn Worldwide and we will forward your request. Both the author and publisher appreciate hearing from you and learning of your enjoyment of this book and how it has helped you. Llewellyn Worldwide cannot guarantee that every letter written to the author can be answered, but all will be forwarded. Please write to:

Philip Brown
℅ Llewellyn Worldwide
2143 Wooddale Drive, Dept. 0-7387-0992-1
Woodbury, MN 55125-2989, U.S.A.

Please enclose a self-addressed stamped envelope for reply, or $1.00 to cover costs. If outside U.S.A., enclose international postal reply coupon.

Many of Llewellyn's authors have websites with additional information and resources. For more information, please visit our website:

www.llewellyn.com